SMART RETAIL

2nd edition

Books that make you better

Books that make you better. That make you *be* better, *do* better, *feel* better. Whether you want to upgrade your personal skills or change your job, whether you want to improve your managerial style, become a more powerful communicator, or be stimulated and inspired as you work.

Prentice Hall Business is leading the field with a new breed of skills, careers and development books. Books that are a cut above the mainstream – in topic, content and delivery – with an edge and verve that will make you better, with less effort.

Books that are as sharp and smart as you are.

Prentice Hall Business.
We work harder – so you don't have to.

For more details on products, and to contact us, visit
www.pearsoned.co.uk

Smart retail

How to turn your store into
a sales phenomenon

2nd edition

RICHARD HAMMOND

PEARSON
Prentice Hall
BUSINESS

Harlow, England • London • New York • Boston • San Francisco • Toronto • Sydney • Singapore • Hong Kong
Tokyo • Seoul • Taipei • New Delhi • Cape Town • Madrid • Mexico City • Amsterdam • Munich • Paris • Milan

PEARSON EDUCATION LIMITED

Edinburgh Gate
Harlow CM20 2JE
Tel: +44 (0)1279 623623
Fax: +44 (0)1279 431059
Website: www.pearsoned.co.uk

First published in Great Britain in 2003
Second edition published 2007

© Pearson Education Limited 2003, 2007

The right of Richard Hammond to be identified as author of this work has been
asserted by him in accordance with the Copyright, Designs and Patents Act 1988

ISBN: 978-0-273-71277-0

British Library Cataloguing-in-Publication Data
A catalogue record for this book is available from the British Library

Library of Congress Cataloging-in-Publication Data
Hammond, Richard.
   Smart retail: how to turn your store into a sales phenomenon/Richard
Hammond.—2nd ed.
      p. cm.
   ISBN-13: 978-0-273-71277-0 (pbk.)
1. Retail trade—Management.   I. Title.
   HF5429.H2824 2007
   658.8'7–dc22   2007033186

10 9 8 7 6 5 4 3 2 1
11 10 09 08 07

Typeset by 3
Printed by Ashford Colour Press Ltd, Gosport

The publisher's policy is to use paper manufactured from sustainable forests.

Smart
retail

. . . is still dedicated to customers – the people who pay our wages.

Contents

Acknowledgements ix

Photo acknowledgements x

Introduction to the second edition xi

Preface – retail thrills xiii

Simplicity xvi

How to accelerate with *Smart Retail* xix

Part one   YOU
Let's get down to business

1 Money where your mouth is 3

2 Rising above the crowd 9

3 Rolling those snowballs 13

Part two   TEAM
Make us happy and we will make you money

4 What's the Big Idea? 23

5 How to build great teams 27

6 How to get people out of bed 55

7 All we need is a little better every time 69

Part three   CUSTOMER
Make me happy and I will give you my money

8 How to make more money 85

9 Great customer service 91

10 A little bit about strategy and why it's worth bothering

reading about 107

11 Promote or die 125

12 Marketing for real people 137

13 A brief history of retail 149

Part four STORE
Surprise and delight to put more money in the till

14 Discovery! 173

15 The great big theatre of shop 187

16 Store environment 193

Epilogue – and we're done? 199

Appendices

Appendix I – Take action 202

Appendix II – Street Time 204

Appendix III – Books for retailers 207

Index 209

Acknowledgements

For the second edition

Thank you so much to all the retailers and friends who so kindly gave me your feedback – it's all been so valuable. Thanks especially to Mark, Melanie, Will, Russ, Chris, TT and Rocky who have been there with ideas, suggestions and the offer of a beer many times when the going has been tough. And a really big thank you to Samantha Jackson at Pearson for her patience and support. Good stuff!

For the first edition

A retail career takes us away from our family and friends for huge chunks of time. To be a retailer is impossible without the dedicated support of the people we love. I have been so lucky to have a wonderful family supporting me in all those twists and turns that a life in retail offers.

I would like to say thank you to those inspirational friends who have made retail so rewarding for me. First to Umesh Vadodaria and Mahendra Patel for making me get off my bum and do things. To 'Buffalo' Steve Smith for that very first break at 16. To Glyn Moser for making me see how important people are. To Janet for the belief that I could get the things in my head out and down on paper. To Rachael Stock at Pearson for making this book better than I had imagined it could be. Thank you also to all the many retailers who gave up time, advice and ideas for *Smart Retail* – you know who you are and you are all superstars.

I would like to add this last thing: all the effort, sacrifice, set-backs and challenges have been worth it. Retail is the best life in the world.

Photo acknowledgements

6 421315 >

The publisher would like to thank the following for their kind permission to reproduce their photographs:

p.v, 21, 35, 64, 94, 126, 176: Koworld; p.83: Bowbrick/Creative Commons Licence; p.105: Elaine Guy; p.146 Andrea Cohen; p.156: RIBA Library Photographs Collection: Royal Institute of British Architects; p.159: A&P Historical Society; p.161: PA Photos/AP; p.163: PA Photos/Heribet Proepper/AP; p.166: Bobak Ha'Eri; p.168: National Portrait Gallery, London; p.171: MPREIS: Thomas Jantscher http://www.jantscher.ch/web02e/index.cfm; p.200: Stillwater Rock

Every effort has been made to trace the copyright holders and we apologise in advance for any unintentional omissions. We would be pleased to insert the appropriate acknowledgement in any subsequent edition of this publication.

Introduction to the second edition

Hi, welcome to the second edition of *Smart Retail*. It's been a cracking four years since the first edition and I'd like to kick off this new version with a massive thank you to all the retailers who provided such kind and useful feedback: thanks for the ideas, I've listened and incorporated many of your suggestions.

Last time, I concentrated on the critical area of teams and how they can create fantastic customer experiences. This time around I've been able to significantly expand on the areas of format, promotion and service quality. I've learnt a lot since 2003 (and hope to go on learning for as long as I breathe) and in particular it's become clear to me that all retail, all shopping, is absolutely about discovery. Few retailers currently exploit that truth effectively – this edition contains all you need to change that. Discovery is a big deal and I'm looking forward to hearing how you take up the idea and improve your businesses with it.

I wanted the new edition to be useful to previous readers of the book as well as for newcomers and so, as well as the crucial stuff on discovery, I've rewritten pretty much everything else – new case studies, new examples, clearer explanations and many whole new chapters. I've also had the opportunity to add a section on retail history – this stuff is important and as I enjoy my twenty-first year in retail I realise that so many situations today are directly mirrored in experiences the retail pioneers went through. There are answers there to modern challenges and it's well worth tipping our caps to those retail kings and revisiting their genius for our own benefit.

That there internet thing

Nowhere in the book do I make much distinction between retailing on the internet and retailing in a store – and that's because they are the *same* activity. Both are about selling products people want in nice, shoppable environments – supported by robust systems, great customer service and effective communications. Retail standards apply in the same way across both forms.

Where distinctions do apply is in the suitability of your product, positioning and format to either form. The rule of thumb is this: if you are a bricks and mortar retailer then you are unwise to be without a credible online outlet – it's another store and one with a big potential catchment area. However, it's less clear cut the other way round: the internet allows smaller retailers to reach far more people, more directly and more powerfully than a few physical stores might.

As internet retailing has matured, so too has an acceptance that both forms can learn from each other. Internet retailers have begun to understand better the principles of the complete customer experience, while bricks and mortar retailers have slowly begun to learn how to communicate better and how to give customers more reasons to come back. Reminding us that they exist, telling us about good things we might like to buy and reminding us to come visit is something the best internet retailers do superbly well – better than any high street store. Internet retailers say 'thank you' better than traditional ones too – and that's more powerful than you might think.

Preface – retail thrills

One thing that hasn't changed since the first edition is that retail is still physically and mentally hard work. Non-retailers find that hard to believe, but with constant pressure on our shoulders, we're only ever as good as our last trading day. Every time we open the store what follows could be a disaster or a triumph.

And that's the thrill of thing, that's why we do it: getting things right, getting the team pulling together, making customers happy and taking some money ... those are the days that keep us coming back for more. Getting retail right is thrilling, magic even.

Getting retail right is thrilling, magic even.

Welcome then to *Smart Retail*, where together we can try to make sure that you enjoy more good days, better profits, a happier team, an improved business performance and a boost to your retail career. I love selling things in shops – it is my passion – and this book is all about sharing retail excellence so that we can all enjoy the good bits of it more often.

Asking the questions

Both editions of *Smart Retail* have been put together on the back of one simple question that I've asked the world's best retailers: 'What makes you so good?' Maybe it's a surprise that they would reveal the answer to that question. That they have, over and over, is, I think, because great retailers have a passion not just for their own success but a belief that the more retail businesses that get it right, the better off we all become. That's a fundamental component of economic growth – retail plays a critical role in the success of economies, and the UK, in particular, owes much of its last decade of success to the superb performance of some of the best retail businesses on the planet.

Because the book is founded on examples of best practice and because, as we will explore later, there are few 'new tricks' in retail, much of what we cover has been done before. I make no secret of that. You will already know lots of it and you will easily understand all of it. This isn't a bullshit fairy-dust consultant's book: this is a collection of answers to your challenges, a professional self-help resource. It's not about doing the impossible and being one of the tiny handful of people who invent something new, it's about helping you to make the best use of your own retail instincts and to benefit from the experiences of others.

Brass tacks

The essence of *Smart Retail* is about helping you to make more money, to win the sales battle, to help you and your team stand out from among more than 300,000 shops in the UK.

Stars of the shop floor

A good store manager can make a huge impact on the success of an individual store, much more so than a clever marketing director or number-lovin' finance chief. With a good manager at the helm, great sales teams can make a big and immediate impact. Although I've presented the ideas here in straightforward terms, that doesn't mean they're not sophisticated; we're talking about best practice learnt from time spent with the world's best retailers – everything here is accessible to store teams and everything is potentially incredibly powerful.

As much as I'd love the bosses to use *Smart Retail* to make positive changes, I'm hoping that grafters right out there on the shop floor will read it too. I've had a lot of feedback from so-called 'lowly' checkout-people and sales assistants who have been inspired by *Smart Retail* to push themselves forward. So much for 'lowly' – I'm really looking forward to the day when my agency rings you up to ask if we can come and work for you and your retail empires. It's been fun writing this second edition but if just one more person, maybe you, uses the book to realise their true retail potential, that's worth more than gold to me.

What's in it for you?

Back in 2003, I wrote that 'we are entering a retail era in which the merchants are back in charge' and it's been fascinating to watch that process unfold – where the real retailers took charge, those retail business have accelerated. Something else has happened too: the barriers to entry for new retail business have dropped a little at the same time as private equity money has made big leaps into the sector. Breakout retailers such as Hotel Chocolat, ASOS.com, Apple and even the cruelly treated Fopp have shown that fresh thinking, passion and retail instinct can shake up existing markets and create huge value.

That gives me masses of hope for your success too. There is nothing to stop you pushing yourself. Good ideas, retail ability and energy are worth money again – use the ideas and strategies in *Smart Retail* to make the breakout and create momentum for yourself.

At the risk of this going a bit Tony Robbins: you can do it!

Now, let's make it happen!

Simplicity

We have this weird natural tendency to assume that success has to be complex, but that's nonsense. Without exception, the world's best retailers do 'simple' brilliantly: they communicate simple ideas clearly and quickly and they meet obvious, straightforward needs in simple, straightforward ways. You need a nicely designed table – you go to Ikea; you need a basic T-shirt – you pick one up while wandering around Tesco; you need a discounted book – you tap its title into Amazon. Well, maybe you don't. Maybe you're spending thousands on tables hewn from the very marble of the Parthenon, but all over the world hundreds of millions of shoppers are responding to the consistently simple propositions of fantastic retailers.

Let's explore that further: having spent time with the world's best retailers one thing shines out from each of them, and that is simplicity. They make it clear what they are for, they sort things out, they make things happen through heavy application of common sense and 'the obvious'. It pains me to see blind retailers drag their businesses through horribly complex processes of organisational change, branding transformation and culture-shifting without really understanding the commonsense issues, and without having a clue who their customers are. And it happens all the time.

I've happily turned down projects with big, lumbering retailers desperate for a bit of consulting 'pixie dust' without being prepared to look at the simple stuff. Those strugglers would often then go on to launch meaningless and wasteful programmes of transformation that only served to deepen the disconnection with customers and the alienation of store staff (who are always more practically minded than their central bosses). The only time these struggles would end was the point at which a new boss arrived with a simple and honest agenda.

When Justin King came to the seriously challenged Sainsbury's in 2003 he found a retailer full of programmes, acronyms, arse-covering, wasteful layers of management and a complete retail paralysis. What was the very first thing King tackled there? On-shelf availability.

always refused the offers of promotion into head office that regularly came his way (including one invite, I remember, that included a retail CEO sending down the company jet to bring MP back for lunch and a chat). I would often, exasperated, tell him he could have been running the whole show. I'll admit that I began to question where exactly Mahendra's passion was.

Then over a meal one evening Mahendra told me: 'I am a teacher, I always was. My job is to make as many people as I possibly can feel that they can be better than they are now, that they can improve their lot. Life is about hope and I've been lucky enough to give some of the people who have worked with me some of that hope.'

I don't think I ever saw MP actually sell anything, but his stores, and regions, always performed better when he was at the helm. MP's passion was for improvement. Not to create teams of sales animals but to make things better – better for colleagues and better for customers. That passion is what makes this retail business great.

2
Rising above the crowd

So with all this bursting passion we have, the next step is to create some action, to make some changes. Let's say you work for Tesco. I'm not suggesting you have to or anything, Tesco is just a good example of a big multiple retailer. If you really did work for Tesco, you would be a single voice among 148,000 colleagues. To accelerate your career, or just to get your good ideas heard, acted upon and producing benefits for the whole business, then you have to raise your profile in the company. You have to become the one in 148,000 who everybody notices.

You have to become the one in 148,000 who everybody notices.

These are my top suggestions for raising your profile in a multiple-store environment.

Volunteer for things

Put your name forward for projects at all levels. You hear that your area manager wants someone to look after a roll out? Stick your hand up for that one. Getting involved will bring you into contact with members of the central marketing team as well as senior operations people.

Such projects often turn out to be good fun, hard work but a nice break from the normal routine. The extra work also gives you a good opportunity to persuade your boss to strengthen your assistant manager positions.

Introduce yourself to people at every meeting

Go up to the MD at the next annual conference and say hello. Tell him or her who you are and where you work. If you have a useful point to make about the business or the presentations you have seen at the conference even better. Try not to corner them though, or you'll get a reputation for being a bit scary.

Make good use of the ideas programme if there is one

If there's a proper ideas programme in place, use it. Put clear, sensible ideas into the programme whenever you can. Make each submission separately – that way you increase your chance of the evaluation committee noticing you.

Give people your mobile phone number

Whenever a senior person comes into your store, engage them. Give them your mobile phone number and mention that you are always happy to have them bounce ideas off you. The best people at head office know the value of having people in the store they can turn to for 'reality checks' on ideas and projects.

Form an opinion

If you have something interesting and cohesive to say, that will help you to appear more credible when you introduce yourself to senior people. Don't be afraid to research and then to rehearse an opinion. Both those things help to make you worth talking to.

Become an expert in a particular area, especially one in which you have experience.

Specialise

Become an expert in a particular area, especially one in which you have experience. Read up on that subject, start to bring it into conversations, let people know that you are an information source and that you are happy to share your knowledge.

Produce the goods

Success does your talking for you: in whatever role you occupy make sure that you are delivering the very best possible performance. That's what this book is for – to give you lots of ways in which to meet and exceed your targets.

3

Rolling those snowballs

Every change has to start somewhere. How do you find that one small thing that can get you on the road to big performance improvement? The good news is that you don't have to change lots of things all in one go to make a difference. Change is about understanding how to spot just one thing to change today.

One thing changed can be the start of something big. Change one detail that one customer notices, who mentions it to five others, who each tell five more, and you can see that one change can make a big impact. Your team also begins to see things starting to happen, just from one idea. Employee attitudes begin to improve. Baby steps: do one thing brilliantly today, another tomorrow and maybe change the world next week. Remember rolling snowballs as a kid? It's like that. You start small and with a bit of effort you soon have something big going on.

> **Baby steps: do one thing brilliantly today, another tomorrow and maybe change the world next week.**

Case study 3.1 Not Smart Retail: Observation, change and simplicity

I have an ongoing row with one of Britain's oldest and biggest, but recently least successful, retailers. It's about simplicity: I meet up with the senior people there every year or so and they are always mired in some crazy consultant-led transformation process or other. Their biggest problem, and they've identified this themselves, is that they don't know who their customers are and so subsequently they don't know what they should be selling or how they should be selling it.

This business tries to solve that problem by trundling off down incredibly twisty roads and arriving, more lost than ever, at crazy conclusions. The one thing they never do? Stand in their stores and watch who comes in. They never talk to their customers face-to-face. Conversations on the spur of the moment can tell you so much. Detailed research is important and useful but it's no replacement for pounding the shop-floor (in your competitors' stores as well as your own) and talking to people.

But this retailer never does that, and it's to their shame – thousands of staff are depending on that management team to provide them with security and opportunity but they are being failed, and have been for years. They're failing customers too – there is an important high-street role for this business and it's been lost while the top team tinkers with over-complex analysis of simple issues.

Too many successes are prevented from happening because a good person cannot make space or time to find their first small change. It's easy to become hidebound by the realities around you. Learning to systematically read a store is an excellent way to break out of that particular rut.

There is an art to reading a store. I should warn you: once you learn to do it systematically, shopping is never the same again. You won't even be able to go into a jumble sale without analysing the store, the staff and the customers. So what's the secret? Well that's it: the store, the staff and the customers. They can tell you what's really happening.

Reading stores

I'll bet good money that you already do this when you walk into a shop: you look around. You look at the fixtures, the offers, the dirt on the carpet and you spot the display gaps. You might even suck your teeth a bit and feel relieved that some other manager is under pressure for once.

Now stand still and observe

Watch where customers are going.

▶ Which part of each section do they enter first?

Look at peoples' eyes.

▶ What do they see?

▶ What do they miss?

What things do they touch?

▶ Which items do they pick up and from where?

▶ How long do customers linger over each display fixture?

How many lookers at each display take something to the counter, or to the changing room?

What sorts of people are shopping in the store? Mums with pushchairs, office workers or mechanics? (This profile will be different at different times of the day.)

Pay special regard to what happens in the transition zone, that area near the door that transfers customers from the outside and then into the store – how do people move through this area?

Most of us make a basic mistake when we shop in our own store. We tend to look at it from back to front. We usually see the store from the back staff area or warehouse through the shopfloor and out of the front doors. It's a natural mistake but incredibly unhelpful. We just aren't seeing the store the way our customers do.

Then take a look at the basic store components

▶ Promotions

▶ Range

▶ Pricing logic

▶ Fixtures and fittings

▶ Lighting layouts

▶ Added-value ideas.

Go through this in your competitors' stores too. I believe firms should not only encourage you to go out reading your competitors' stores but that they should even give you a paid session, every week, to go off and do so. In fact they should even give you a fiver to go get a latte to slurp while you walk around improving your business through learning from your competitors and other retailers.

Staff

Talk to staff every time you go into a shop. An easy icebreaker is to ask 'What's it like working here?' You will usually get a plain answer along the lines of 'It's not too bad', which doesn't tell you much but does give you a chance to then ask 'What do you like about it?' Nearly every time you ask that the assistant will let slip a nugget of useful information:

▶ 'There's a nice team spirit.'

▶ 'The pay is good.'

▶ 'It's a laugh.'

▶ 'We're treated with a bit of respect.'

▶ 'Every day is different.'

▶ 'I like customers.'

Each of those answers allows you to unobtrusively ask further questions that help to get to specific employment practices in play at that store. Try to chat with the store manager too. Tell them what you do. Share some thoughts and ideas and they often will with you.

Customers

Listen

▶ What do customers say to each other?

▶ What do they say to assistants?

▶ How are customers being approached?

Talking to customers in your own store is easy – you've got a badge that says you are okay to talk to. Talking to customers elsewhere is a bit harder to do. Brits tend to be a little wary of strangers asking questions, but it can be done without you appearing to be a nutter. Most people love to share their opinions: turn that to your advantage.

Most people love to share their opinions: turn that to your advantage.

In your own store you can ask lots of open questions

▶ 'How well have we looked after you today?'

▶ 'What do you think about how we've changed our displays?'

▶ 'How easy was it to find what you were looking for?'

▶ 'What do you think of these new products?'

▶ 'How easy is it to shop in my store?'

▶ 'What was the first thing you noticed when you came in today?'

▶ 'What's your opinion on how I've set up my till area?'

▶ 'What am I missing in my store do you think?'

▶ 'What sort of things do other shops like mine do that you really like?'

When I'm in my civvies and out in somebody else's store, I find the most successful question tends to be 'I run a store like this one, what do you like about this shop?' and I'll be asking that usually while waiting in a queue at the tills. Lots of other opportunities to open up a conversation usually present themselves while wandering around the store too.

If the customer starts to chat happily, be conversational and don't try to sound like a survey. People tend to respond along the lines of 'Oh I like the way they do X, but I really wish they would sort out that damn Y'. Maybe we just like complaining but I have found over and over again that these little chats can uncover a glaring problem for you to look out for in your own store. Of course some customers will also happily give you a run down of what it is that attracts them to the particular store you are in and that's extra useful.

Street Time

As a consultancy we do a cracking version of exactly this process: we send teams of senior retailers, each clutching a twenty-pound note to spend, out into shops. We call this programme 'Street Time' and those retailers are targeted with visiting a selected set of stores and reporting back on them. They talk to staff (we've had at least five people hired by our clients after having had great in-store conversations), they talk to customers, occasionally they get escorted out by over-zealous security guards. The most useful part is always, they tell us, the standing back and watching customers bit – we give ourselves that essential time too infrequently.

You'll find the very simple notes for our Street Time exercise in Appendix II – read the sections on big ideas, mission, values and discovery before taking a crack at it.

Turning the things we see into things we do

Reading stores is powerful only if you do it with a purpose. That purpose is to find one thing to change in your own store today. Write down your notes as soon as you can and then do a bit of simple analysis: set up three headings – 'benefit', 'effort' and 'cost'. Mark each idea out of ten for each of those headings and then pick out the ones that look most attractive and get on with them!

All of these you would consider doing

▶ Lots of benefit, easy to do, no cost.

▶ Useful benefit, easy to do, no cost.

▶ Lots of benefit, bit of effort required, some cost.

▶ Useful benefit, bit of effort required, some cost.

These you would not do

▶ Some benefit, easy to do, lots of cost.

▶ Little benefit, hard to do, lots of cost.

Open your eyes and see stuff!

Great retailers think about their worlds differently. I've already gone on a bit about simplicity and passion but that's because these things are so important. I'm going to throw instinct and empathy into that pot now: instinctive understanding of where the real issues are and empathy for the customer experience are incredibly powerful tools.

Instinct, emotion, passion and risk are legitimate decision-making tools in this business: that's a tough concept because it falls quite some distance away from business norms of meticulously researched forecasts, trends and research. Why is that? We're all customers too, we all know what we like and dislike, we instinctively know what's a good idea and what's a poor one. We can feel it – so let's hone those skills and start listening to our instincts.

> **Instinct, emotion, passion and risk are legitimate decision-making tools in this business.**

Retail is simple – what we're trying to do is simple: make some money selling nice things to delighted customers. Where the challenge comes is in determining the degree of success behind that simplicity – we want to sell tens of millions of items to millions of ecstatic customers! There is a process I've seen at work in the world's best retailers – one in which the senior team break rules, try things and think in very simple terms. I've distilled the process into four straightforward steps.

Open your eyes

What really happens in your stores? Walk in your customers' shoes, see things without your agenda getting in the way.

Be human

Analyse what you see not in terms of finance, stock-turn or established retail best-practice, but as a human being. What makes you feel happy in this space? What are your needs? What frustrates you? What do you miss?

Interpret what you see and feel

Think about what you've seen and how it affected you. Look at how these things might improve, change or otherwise empower your stores. Can you apply your human interpretation of what you see into a clear solution? Can you unclutter your thoughts and let your instinct guide you?

Make it happen

Write a simple action plan – what, who and when ... and get on with it!

PART TWO – **TEAM**

Make us happy and we will make you money

Picture: Koworld

CHAPTER FOUR

What's the Big Idea?

Before we can start thinking about asking our teams to do anything, we need to know what we are, what we stand for and how we want to behave as a business. The very first stage in doing that is to work out what our Big Idea is. Every great retail business is built around a big idea – a reason for existing, the thing that business is for. It informs absolutely everything that business does and says and informs every decision made within it.

Every great retail business is built around a big idea.

I'd like to thank inspirational markeeter Martin Butler, boss of retail branding business RPM3, for helping me to get this concept into focus (by which I mean he slapped me about a bit and forced me back to the simple and straightforward stuff after I suffered a bout of 'the consultings').

The best way to illustrate this one is to take you through a bunch of examples, starting with Wal-Mart and Target. But just to be extra clear about what I mean by Big Idea, let's look at Wal-Mart's which is 'We are the home of everyday low prices'. That's Wal-Mart's reason-for-being and it's an idea that customers and staff alike understand utterly and fundamentally. It is the big idea that has driven Sam Walton's company since the moment he articulated it one day when he did a bulk deal on ladies' pants and realised he could be more competitive by passing on the savings to customers.

In these examples I'm going to compare two retailers each time to show you how each big idea can be used to create identity but also to exploit opportunity. Again, a nice and easy example before we kick off properly: Thorntons' big idea is 'the specialist chocolates shop', whereas Hotel

Chocolat's big idea is 'the authentic chocolatier'. And it translates as: Thorntons – nice shop full of lovely chocolates, Hotel Chocolat – upmarket shop full of authentic posh chocolate treats. The difference is subtle but consistent – to the customer Thorntons appears to be about volume and convenience, where Hotel Chocolat is about indulgence and authenticity.

Price and value

Wal-Mart – We are the home of everyday low prices

Target – From us you can expect more but still pay less

That's two retailers in the same space – can you see how the subtle shift in Target's big idea might influence how the store is merchandised, ranged and operated? Wal-Mart make a very clear statement of intent with their big idea, but can 'Everyday low prices' also mean 'Lowest price regardless'? I think it can and certainly Target decided that's what it meant. 'Expect More. Pay Less.' still makes a very strong statement about price but also makes it clear that there are gems to be discovered at Target. And it's worked – Wal-Mart have seen off Woolworths and to a large extent K-Mart too, but Target have flourished by filling in the gaps left behind by Wal-Mart's very certain positioning.

Store or brand?

Selfridges & Co – The house of brands

Harrods – The world's most exclusive store

The resurgence of Selfridges came when they stopped thinking about 'Selfridges' as important and concentrated on brands – creating a house of brands and then presenting those brands with drama, surprise, excitement, noise and theatre. Harrods on the other hand has clung to promoting the store itself as the raison d'etre – and that's had the effect of making it feel just a little naff, a bit touristy. Visitors 'do' Harrods when they come to London. Harrods does have a big idea but hasn't yet realised that it's perhaps the wrong one. Same applies to Macy's in New York – a store resting so heavily on its laurels that it may well sink.

No Big Idea

WHSmith is a fascinating case because the retail company actually consists of two separate businesses: WHSmith High Street and WHSmith Travel (which isn't a travel bookshop but rather the WHSmith stores you see at airports and train stations all over the world).

WHSmith stock books, magazines, cards, sweets, stationary, DVDs, music and gifts. On the high street it leads in just one sector – there are better stationers, better book stores, and better music shops; only the magazine section is a leading department. It is a high street business that for ten years has had no real idea of what it's actually for. Nobody inside the company actually knows – I've asked.

But WHSmith Travel is brilliant – it's basically the same departments but featuring the highlights. So you'll have top books with some eclectic promotions; a great range of magazines, batteries, film and camera memory cards; sweets and drinks and headache tablets. Its big idea is to reliably equip every traveller with everything they could want to make their journey a better one. The ranges are perfect, the merchandising spot-on and the till-process efficient and pleasant. The big idea guides everyone: you know exactly what to look out for as a buyer, exactly what to range as a marketeer and exactly how to present it as a merchandiser. You know because the big idea is so clear it drives an obvious and practical mission.

Taking on the established giant and turning their big idea in on itself

IKEA – Honest furniture for all

ILVA – We believe in value. But 'value' is often confused with 'cheap'. Good value is high quality and good service with low cost. Cheap is just low quality at low cost. Good value lasts. Cheap will do for now.

You can see Danish furniture retailer ILVA trying to position itself relative to IKEA in the same way that Target sits inside Wal-Mart's gaps. That big idea at ILVA is expressed, essentially, as a direct poke in IKEA's eye. It's clever and powerful in that it is a challenge to customers for them to progress from the 'Cheap will do for now' IKEA mentality and come to ILVA instead. They are presenting products in the same democratising design way IKEA do, but suggesting that customers express themselves in a more grown-up, more permanent way. It's early days for ILVA in the UK but the signs are positive.

Your Big Idea

What's the big idea that drives your retail business? Is it clear? Does it make sense? How does it position you relative to the market and to your competitors? If you're the top person at your place and you answer 'no' or 'don't know' to any of these questions please stop reading and sort it out now. Without that clear understanding of what your business is for – well, there's nothing we can do for you!

CHAPTER FIVE

How to build great teams

Happy teams make you more money. The best customer service is delivered by happy, motivated teams. You cannot be a great retail business, long term, in this market without happy and motivated teams. The best performance improvement strategy I could ever recommend to you is 'make your team happy'.

A happy team of friendly, motivated people, pulling together, having fun with customers, bristling with ideas and enthusiasm, full of passion for the job can build huge performance improvements. Like so much in retail, the recommendation to create a happy team is very, very obvious but is also a massive challenge. The best of us still struggle to get every new hire right, to always make the best decision in a given situation, to not drop the ball when the going gets tough. Management is hard to do right: that's why business rates good managers as assets.

Because managing people is hard, great teams are still the exceptions, not the rule. That's actually a good thing for you. Think about it: if most retail teams are not bonding to aid performance, then working hard to create a great team in your store will put you ahead of all those other stores where the team is not so strong. Think of it as competitive advantage through team building.

A consistency I've seen in great retail businesses is that they tend to be very clear on what the business is trying to do (mission), they allow people to behave like grown-ups (respect) and they are very good at recognising positive behaviours (recognition). Let's call them corner-stones: Mission – Respect – Recognition. Wherever the three are in evidence, great team and store cultures emerge and I firmly believe that this *is* a bit of a secret, if there are such things, of great leadership:

▶ **Cornerstone 1**   Mission: We understand what we want to do for our customers.

▶ **Cornerstone 2**   Respect: We make sure our people know they are empowered to do those things.

▶ **Cornerstone 3**   Recognition: We reinforce those positive things by recognising them when they happen.

These three exist as a sort of self-reinforcing loop: the clearer we are about what our business is for, and the better we enable our people to do those things, and the more we notice and say 'thank you' when they do them, then the better we become.

I'll go into each cornerstone in more detail over the next few pages but first I want to illustrate the value and importance of a great store culture. I would also like to show you that your individual store culture can still be a great one even if the wider company culture isn't.

Leadership

Things get a little bit tricky when we start to think about leadership and teams. I have a heartfelt belief that leadership cannot be taught – indeed we once lost out on a large bit of consultancy business because I funda-mentally disagreed with the notion that it could be taught. A UK retailer with 1,300 stores was looking to improve store cultures and were very proud of the expensive leadership programme they had pushed 1,300 man-agers through. But when we peeled back the detail of what had actually happened it became clear that any gains they'd seen as a result of this lead-ership programme were pretty much down to the fact that those 1,300 managers had spent two days out of their businesses and were hyper-aware that senior people were watching them like hawks post-course. It was also clear that those gains would evaporate quite quickly. And here's where we lost the relationship: I'm not sure that the role of Human Resources is to teach a fundamental in-the-genes skill such as leadership: I believe HR's job is to find the existing 1,300 leaders out there within the 48,000-strong workforce and then to put those natural leaders in the right roles. Pointing that out led to a huge disconnect with that particular client, and we've not been back since. When I say 'disconnect' I do, of course, mean hissy fit.

So, do you have to be a good leader to be a great retailer? Do you have to be a good leader to create a strong store culture? The painful answer is that to a large degree, yes, you do. You might want to do a bit of soul-searching for a moment on that. It might help if I define leadership – it's really about answering one question: are you able to inspire others to line up behind your chosen course of action?

Now – having gotten you through that (I'm hoping you answered 'yes') we get to the notion that great leaders can, and sometimes do, still fall on their arses. Being able to lead is essential to the job at hand but understanding where to lead and how to structure the journey are essential too. And that's where your Mission – Respect – Recognition cornerstones come in handy. It's like a leadership map: follow those steps and you'll get to where you want to go.

Let's look at why it's worth making a great store culture one of your destinations.

Why bother?

Cost savings

▶ Reduced shrinkage – happy people don't steal from you and they care more about reducing customer theft as well.

▶ Reduced employee turnover – happy people, and people who feel valued, stay with you longer and that means savings not only on advertising for replacements but also on training and your time.

> **Customers prefer to be served by happy, friendly people: every observational study proves that conclusively.**

Improved customer service

Customers prefer to be served by happy, friendly people: every observational study proves that conclusively. Tied in to the improvements in employee retention are corresponding improvements in employee effectiveness and knowledge. People who stay with you longer tend to get better at their jobs and that filters through directly to the customer experience.

▶ Customers come back more often and they shout about you.

▶ Customers return to stores that feel good to be in – the human dynamic is what sets that atmosphere.

▶ Customers share their great experiences, most of which relate to how your people have looked after them.

Walking the talk

We cover values and mission statements later (don't yawn, we're talking practical advice not management consultant waffle) when I'll explain why these are so important to the success of your business. A great store culture makes an excellent starting point for making values and mission statements really work for you. Walking the talk also means that new ideas tend to be adopted more readily and more happily by the team, everybody is up for driving the team forwards.

Support

You could create a happy team by letting everyone run riot, throw sickies whenever they wanted and help themselves to whatever they fancied from the stock room. That of course wouldn't do anything for the performance of the business. A great store culture still encompasses the unpleasant things such as sacking people who don't make the grade, and reprimanding staff when they let the team down. However, if you have got that great culture built and you have a happy team, they will tend to be far more supportive of you in those difficult decisions. That's useful because it helps keep the disruption of such moments down to a minimum and the team gets over it more quickly.

Enjoyment

Happy teams are nicer to work in. Fun is a powerful component in a high-performing team. In all but a few circumstances customers like getting to go out and buy stuff, so it's reasonable to aim for a fun store culture too.

Fun is a powerful component in a high-performing team.

Reasons not to?

A lot of managers say 'the company culture is so awful that I can't make a difference here in my store'. While I'm sympathetic to the additional pressure a bad company culture puts on its store managers, I can't accept this as a real excuse to avoid building a great store culture. Retail superstar Julian Richer has this to say about the ability of a store manager to lead culture in their own store: 'the culture of the store is determined by the manager, and then we try to get our company culture on top of that'. It's managers who create the store culture, not head office.

Why assistant managers must become 'keepers' of the culture

Richer also remarked that 'it is sad whenever a store manager leaves'. It is indeed sad when a great store manager leaves, and it can often mean the death of a team. This is why store managers should work closely with their assistant managers in planning and building a great culture. Aim to leave a little bit of yourself behind so that whoever takes over, ideally your ASM, can strengthen the culture further, building on your work. For most of us, and I include myself in this, there is massive pleasure to be had from discovering that something you helped build is still solid and in play years later.

Evidence

Many of the case studies in *Smart Retail* show what happens when great store cultures are built. Have a look in particular at the Stew Leonard's story in the Discovery chapter (Case Study 14.1).

Service Profit Chain

I'm not keen on theory for its own sake and I get irritated by diagrams that have more to do with consultants trying to be clever than making a clear point, and that's why there's just the one diagram in the whole of this book.

It's a pretty important one though – some years ago I was introduced to the basic idea that within retail and service organisations it's employees who have the biggest impact on customers' experience of the brand. Sounds obvious when you put it like that and it's true. What Service Profit Chain theory does is turn the fluffy bit of that equation into a way to measure the pound note impact of treating your employees with respect, care and integrity.

Nice means profit

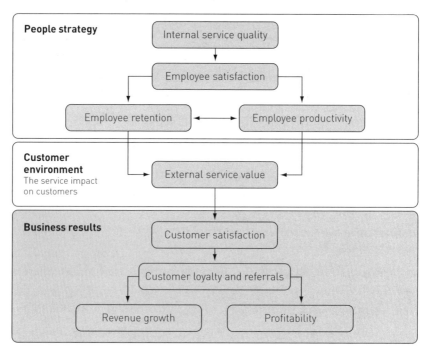

Smart Circle Limited adapted from Heskett

Lets step through those boxes

Internal service quality

▶ Treating your people well is good

Employee satisfaction

▶ because happy, motivated and respected staff are more satisfied

Employee retention

▶ they stay longer with you

Employee productivity

▶ they get better at their jobs

External service value

▶ and happy, stable and productive teams tend to deliver the best customer service experiences

Customer satisfaction

▶ which makes customers jolly happy

Customer loyalty and referrals

▶ and they come back more often, spend more dosh with you and they recommend you to their pals

Revenue growth

▶ which means you stuff your tills with wads of cash

Profitability

▶ which carries on until we all start to have baths filled with money instead of Matey.

And the thing is, the logic of this process is inescapable and can be seen at work inside the world's best retailers, yet it's rarer than it should be. Putting misson, respect and recognition at the heart of your management style will deliver this good stuff. Great employment experiences drive great customer experiences and that probably equals Ferraris all round.

The three cornerstones

Let's just recap on those three cornerstones I mentioned earlier:

▶ **Cornerstone 1** Mission: We understand what we want to do for our customers.

▶ **Cornerstone 2** Respect: We make sure our people know they are empowered to do those things.

▶ **Cornerstone 3** Recognition: We reinforce those positive things by recognising them when they happen.

Now on to the detail!

Cornerstone one: mission

Practical people slaving away at the coalface have a rational dislike of mission statements. We tend to think of them as nothing more than marketing waffle. I suspect that's because we've been subjected to so many awful mission statements that just didn't mean anything. That's a shame because a good mission statement is an incredibly powerful tool. It becomes a rallying point for the whole team.

Has your company got a mission statement? If it has, does it make sense? Does it make clear what it is that the business wants you to do? Does it help you to make choices and decisions? Above all does it reflect the Big Idea? If the answer to those questions is 'no' then you are going to need to rewrite the mission statement yourself. Once you've done that you must make that statement live and breathe; refer to it in every team meeting and offer up every decision and choice you make against it.

The 'Big Idea' we discussed earlier is closely tied-in to your mission. The mission should be an expression of how you are going to deliver that 'Big Idea'.

Parcel delivery company TNT and Britain during the expansionist reign of Elizabeth the First (honestly!) provide two of my favourite examples of mission statements in action. TNT had a mission statement that read 'To deliver every parcel on time'. Is that blindingly obvious? Yes! What this simple but powerful mission statement did was to focus every member of the business on the company's purpose. 'Will spending millions on our new software update help us to deliver every parcel on time?' If the answer is 'yes' then you get on with the analysis, but if it is 'no' then you have just saved the company from a costly mistake. It always makes me laugh when firms invest millions in things that any bloke off the street could tell them will not support the purpose of the business. Incidentally this mission was later replaced with 'service is our only product.' What the hell does that mean? Have they given up delivering parcels? I'm confused!

My other favourite is the original mission statement, the one that built the first British Empire. Today we might feel a little uncomfortable about aspects of the British naval domination that enabled this tiny country to claim vast swathes of the planet for its own. What is undeniable though is that this was an extraordinary achievement.

British warships sailed the world under a very simple mission statement: 'for the Queen's greater good'. In any given situation British commanders could ask themselves 'If I sink that ship, or make a garrison, or secure this island will it be for the Queen's greater good?' If it was, then they would do it. Simple, clear and effective.

A strong, clear mission statement can be a fantastic tool for improving and securing best performance. Make it simple, obvious, reinforcing; and make sure too that it addresses practical objectives.

Values

This is another area where a lot of awful rubbish has been spouted by management gurus. It means that talking about values can feel a little ridiculous. This is a shame because a set of defined values becomes the

Picture: Koworld

Big idea and mission perfectly expressed right there

practical tool that helps you to apply your mission statement to the everyday running of the store. Where the mission statement tells you what the company does, the values tell you how it wants to go about doing it. They are a reflection of what the company stands for. We're talking about a list of words such as innovative, fun, honest and inspirational. The trick is to mould these values into a set of sentences that tell us how to practically apply the values to the jobs we do every day.

A great way to think about values is to fix in your mind the perfect customer experience in your store – then imagine what five emotions your customers might tell you they felt during that experience. Write down that list of emotions and then ask yourself this question: If my customers leave my store feeling those five things, are they likely to come back again? If the answer is 'yes' then you're on to something good.

Case study 5.1 *Smart Retail*: Words we can live by

Tesco has one of the best-defined mission statements and supporting set of values in retail. They are clear, easy to understand and they are relevant. Tesco has consistently applied the same mission and values throughout its surge forward in British grocery retail. The company now enjoys the number one position in the market place having sat behind Sainsbury's for decades. That is a massive achievement, one which visionary former chairman Lord MacLaurin and the current chief executive, the brilliant merchant Sir Terry Leahy, put down to the Tesco team – all 148,000 of them.

Here is that superb Tesco mission statement (they call it a core purpose but that means the same thing as far as I'm concerned) and its supporting values in full.

Mission statement

'To create value for our customers, to earn their lifetime loyalty.'

Values

We do this by embracing the following values:

▶ No one tries harder for customers.

▶ Understand customers better than anyone.

▶ Be energetic, be innovative and be first for customers.

▶ Use our strengths to deliver unbeatable value to our customers.

▶ Look after our people so they can look after our customers.

Treat people how we like to be treated:

▶ There's only one team ... the Tesco Team.

▶ Trust and respect each other.

▶ Strive to do our very best.

▶ Give support to each other and praise more than criticise.

▶ Ask more than tell, and share knowledge so that it can be used.

▶ Enjoy work, celebrate success and learn from experience.

See how they have split the values into those that relate directly to the customer and then those that relate to the team. That's an unusual but useful split. From experience I can tell you that it makes defining your values easier to do. Consider making the same distinction as you build your own set of values.

Using the emotions test, Tesco appears to hope that with a good in-store experience, its customers leave stores feeling: satisfied (no one tries harder), understood (understand customers), surprised (be innovative and be first), saved money (deliver unbeatable value), respected (look after our people so they can look after our customers). If a customer leaves a store feeling satisfied, understood, pleasantly surprised and respected and having spent less than they might have had to elsewhere – are they coming back again? Getting the mission and values right and then living and breathing them affects customers' experiences directly. It's the Service Profit Chain in action.

Walking the talk

Defining a good mission statement and then living the values in-store – or 'walking the talk' – is good for you because it improves the customer experience and builds stronger teams, which in turn increases business performance. In a case such as Tesco, walking the talk in-store is doubly powerful because everything the central team does, such as advertising, promotions, store investment, is also right in line with the mission and values. They strengthen each other.

If you work in a business that has a clear and consistent set of values, use them to your advantage. Live and breathe them, 'walk the talk' – it will improve performance. In an independent store you too must define a mission and a set of values; everything else flows from them them.

A strong mission statement and good set of values reads like the Tesco one, in language that a normal person can easily make sense of. Simple things – strongly stated.

Case study 5.2 *Smart Retail*: Values in action at a leading fashion store

Here is a solid, practical example of the way in which values can make a significant difference to the everyday functioning of your shop. This case study is about a British clothes retailer. One of the very obvious values that applied to this business was that buying or selling clothes was about fun; it's a fun thing to do. Customers wanted a happy environment and staff wanted to enjoy their jobs. In fact that was one of the things that people told us had attracted them to the business; working in fashion retail looked like it might be more fun than stacking shelves. So we included fun as a value. It really supported the company mission too. That mission statement read: 'To delight our customers by giving them affordable access to great high street fashion.'

Fun is a value that many people believe should be part of the working environment for almost any retailer, and I agree. I don't mean mindless larking about but the generation of genuine 'this is cool' moments for customers and staff alike. Fun helps make shopping enjoyable. We are all in the business of making shopping fun, whether we are selling washing machines or watches.

Fun with job descriptions

One of my favourite methods for making values work every day in-store is to rewrite job descriptions. Out goes the dry HR-speak and in comes practical stuff about what to do and why. In the case of this retailer we had identified one particular group of employees who were really hard to engage. There was a set of 16 to 18-year-old girls who all worked one weekday evening and then all day Saturday. They are notoriously hard to engage, as you hardly see them all week then suddenly they are there on your busiest day when you've got little time to give them. It's crucial that you have these girls on board and pulling for the team, or they can become a disruptive and negative element in the store. They are also famous for micky-taking, degrees of lateness and for being uncommitted when they do finally arrive. This was especially true on hung-over Saturday mornings!

We looked at their job descriptions which – and to be honest I can't blame them – I doubt any of the girls themselves had read. One of the most important responsibilities, in fact the first task they were supposed to perform on Saturday mornings, read like this: 'You will ensure all merchandise rails, shelves and/or islands are fully filled and merchandised in accordance with the prevailing marketing planogram for your store grade and profile.' Of course what this actually meant was simply 'Make sure there are no gaps on display when we let the punters in.' The girls regarded this responsibility as a real chore: boring. Not the sort of thing they wanted to do when arriving tired after a big Friday night out.

So we changed it, we introduced that value of fun. The same line from the job description now read 'Fashion is fun – remember that as you dive into the stockroom and pull out your favourite, most exciting fashions. We want you to take your choices, the clothes you think customers should be wearing out tonight, onto the sales-floor. Get them onto the racks, anywhere there are gaps, and get your choices noticed.' When we trialled it the effect was fantastic.

Because we had asked the girls to think for themselves – and who really is best placed to say what the trendiest clothes are for 16 to 18-year-old girls than a group of 16 to 18-year-old girls – they actually got excited by the task, even beginning to come in early to get the best picks. They also got competitive with each other and would jostle for space and monitor each others' selections like hawks. Very healthy stuff indeed, with the unexpected side effect that the girls also began to sell proactively. They would make sure every customer saw their personal picks and they would ensure that a constant supply of sizes and colours was always out on display. That's how a mission statement and a clear set of values can have a direct effect on the performance of the team.

Street Time

Now that you've read about big ideas, mission, values and discovery, please have a look at the Street Time tool in Appendix II. As well as being good fun to do, it's something that will help you to go out and find many ways to improve and change your business.

Cornerstone two: respect

'Treat people how you yourself would wish to be treated'. My Nan used to say that to me and, like a lot of the wisdom of her generation, it's absolutely on the money. In today's retail landscape you have no option but to treat your people with respect. Here's why . . .

A disrespectful market

The mobile phone retail business enjoyed, or suffered, a yo-yo sales curve during the 1990s and into the 2000s. Excellent businesses such as Carphone Warehouse were not immune when the market first dipped sharply. But when picture messaging and colour-screen phones (those things feel like they came along decades not mere years ago, don't they?) sent the mobile phone market back upwards, Carphone Warehouse benefited more than most. Carphone Warehouse is the honest phone retailer that emerged out of a time when the sector was dominated by sharks and cowboys. This is a retailer that prides itself on looking after everybody's needs; customers and staff alike. It is a retailer whose successful employment policy is built on respect. It is also a retailer that has benefited from the very positive knock-on effects of such a policy.

Talk to an employee of Carphone Warehouse and they will tell you that the work is hard, the hours long and that the standards are stretching and rigorously applied. They will also tell you that they enjoy it enormously. Push a little harder and ask them 'Why do you enjoy it here?' and a consistent story emerges:

- ▶ 'We get treated with respect.'
- ▶ 'I'm trained so well that I never look stupid in front of customers.'
- ▶ 'My ideas are worth something.'
- ▶ 'I'm allowed, no I'm encouraged, to use my brain.'
- ▶ 'It's made clear that I can have a proper career at Carphone Warehouse if I want one.'

By 2003 the bad times appeared to have gone and the future looked bright again for mobile phone retailers. Carphone Warehouse had weathered the storm because they had looked after customers and employees. The respect they show to staff is visible in the respect staff show to customers. As a result, the majority of customers stayed with the Carphone Warehouse business through the bad times even though they knew they could buy the same phone cheaper elsewhere.

An alternative approach can be seen in the same marketplace: back in 2003 Phones 4U featured in a fascinating TV documentary. In one now infamous scene a manager was shown enjoying the dubious honour of receiving what could be considered as quietly threatening phone calls from the then millionaire chairman John Caudwell. These phone calls were to remind that manager that he had but one week to improve the numbers or face the sack. That's a classic example of management by fear rather than management by respect. I asked Phones 4U how they felt about the picture portrayed in that documentary. They told me the result had been an upsurge in job applications from people they called 'real go-getters, the sort of people who respond to a bit of pressure'.

When I wrote the first edition of *Smart Retail* I said I was keen to see how this attitude would pan out for customers over the long term. The short answer is that Carphone Warehouse ran away with the prize, John Caudwell sold Phones 4U (for a tidy profit, mind) and the business has spent the last two years working hard to improve its customer service standards as well as improving the way it manages its people. And guess what – it's working, but perhaps too slowly to dent Carphone Warehouse's lead significantly.

The failure of fear

In a fast-growing market where price and availability are the overriding considerations, many customers will happily buy from the cheapest outfit regardless of reputation. The situation then changes quickly when market conditions tighten and saturation is reached. In the slowdown, customers gravitate to quality, they think a little more carefully about what they want and they look for reliable sources of good advice. Then, when things begin to pick up again, customers often stick with the new relationships they've formed. They value relationships with retailers who have looked after them knowledgeably, honestly and with a smile. More than that – in an era in which customers have lots of choice they tend to vote with their feet and go where the best experiences are overall.

Back in the 1980s there was a surge in consumer spending. In the UK this surge ran alongside unprecedented levels of unemployment – for some everything was rosy and for others desperate. A group of UK retailers became incredibly successful because of the surge but some also chose to profit from the high levels of unemployment and to exploit their work-forces. With demand for fashion, food and consumer goods at times outstripping supply, leading stores were able to sell almost everything they could display. The best firms looked after their staff well and saw back-ground unemployment as a reason to be a *good* employer rather than a bad one. The flip side was some retailers saw people as disposable, an expend-able resource to be bullied into line. Customers were blind to the effects of this as they scrambled over themselves to buy, buy, buy and so the bully-boy retailers got away with treating staff badly.

A management style grew up in that time called JFDI, or 'just flipping do it' (you and I both know that I've changed one of those words to a print-friendly alternative). JFDI was anti-respect, it was all about conformity and subservience. I first entered retailing in the middle of this period and it was mean at times. Nasty even. It was an atmosphere that chewed people up, burnt them out, took advantage of job insecurity and made some people's lives horrid.

By the early 1990s the boom and bust cycle was beginning to flatten, along with a calming of rabid consumerism and large reductions in levels of unemployment – a longer-term sustainable prosperity was established. And something happened in the way people, especially in the UK, shopped: they became more discerning, as if the hangover of the '80s was accompanied by an understanding that spending for the sake of spending wasn't a great idea anymore.

Customers appeared to begin to notice that those businesses run on the principles of JFDI weren't nice places to shop. They moved away from them in significant volumes – and would even ridicule the experiences to be had in those old-school bully-led businesses. Customers aren't stupid: they might not be able to define what it is that they notice in a JFDI-led store but it does affect them.

This effect is just one very good reason for investing in and showing respect for your staff. Forget even the straightforward cost benefits of keeping your staff longer, the simple reality is that teams built on respect and passion ultimately bring more profit into your business. Teams built on fear and unreasonable pressure do often create short-term sales gains but they always crack, and usually this happens very quickly. What is more, they leave customers feeling negative about their interaction with the brand and less inclined to ever come back again. In an age of real-time access to live sales numbers it can be easy to fall back, under pressure, into a JFDI management style. Don't. What your business gains today it will lose tomorrow and next week.

> **Teams built on respect and passion ultimately bring more profit into your business.**

The respect deal

Respect, thankfully, is a two-way street. Yes you will still have to deal with underperforming colleagues. Yes you might find yourself having to exit people from your business. That is always hard to do, but in a team that has been built on respect you will have worked hard with that person to make things right. The people in your team will know that and will support your decisions rather than becoming unsettled by them.

'You have to earn respect' is a well-known phrase, and in retail management that gets warped a little. *You*, as a manager, have to earn respect from your team – sure – but you must unquestioningly respect *them* from day one! People are always wary of change, which is why you will have to work hard to earn their respect. But this is not a mutual deal. Even before you first meet your team you have to respect them. If you didn't, if you came into a new store with an attitude that said 'I'm in charge and until I know you I am reserving my judgement' then people tend to turn off.

Luckily, the most effective way to earn respect is to give it! If you systematically go about building trust, recognising people's contributions, sharing training and creating opportunities for personal growth then you will build a strong, successful team that likes and respects you. You will have gone a long way to building a brilliant culture.

For some great tips on how to build respect read Chapter 6 which is about motivation. I've listed a whole series of them there.

Case study 5.3 Smart Retail: Top Shop – instinct, respect and risk

'I have this thing about men in suits you know, people who drone on about the principles of retail. What bollocks. There aren't any principles of retailing.'[1]

Jane Shepherdson – former Brand Director[2], Top Shop

Top Shop is the British retailer born as a concession in a Sheffield department store in 1964. Gloriously it has never held itself to be anything more than a store selling cheap and cheerful clothes to young women. Shepherdson took on the top job in 1999 – Top Shop's thirty-fifth year – and transformed it utterly, not in terms of market position or, necessarily, the type of clothes it sells, but by making the store exciting, unpredictable, passionate and anti-marketing. By that I mean that she has drilled into her entire team that they must ignore the rules and do what feels natural instead. This was, at the time, a huge risk – a proper gamble.

Top Shop's big idea is brilliantly simple: be our own customers, forget the needs of the business. That's shocking but it's an attitude, a revolution indeed, that has put Top Shop among the world's most high-profile and successful retailers.

Here's an example of how Jane forced the rules to be broken by thinking like customers: *'I would go into meetings and say "Yes, I know that's selling and it's selling two thousand units but I don't care, it's awful and we're not going to buy awful things any more regardless of whether or not they will sell." If you're going to earn people's trust, you have to set a standard. That set the standard – all the buyers now know that, and all the buyers now stand by every single thing in their range. Compare this to ten or twenty years ago when some buyers would sit there saying, "Have you seen this, isn't it horrible? Guess how many we sold last week ... isn't that great?" I thought it was outrageous. How could they do that? It's not right, there's no integrity.'*

How often have you dropped a profitable product because you don't think your customers should be buying it? 'Never' is the answer for most of us. What that kind of thinking has done at Top Shop, together it has to be said with modern just-in-time logistics allowing fast stock turn, is to create a store that feels utterly in tune with customers. It's risk that is at the heart of that transformation.

The power of standing for something, of building the retail business around that big idea, then living and breathing it, is the best kept secret in retailing. It's a passionate, instinctive thing and at the heart of every successful retail business.

[1] The Jane Shepherdson quotes in this case study are based on an interview in Martin Butler's essential book on retailing, *People Don't Buy What You Sell (They Buy What You Stand For)*.

[2] Although Jane moved on from Top Shop in 2006, there is absolutely no doubt that the incredible continued success there is directly attributable to her revolution, attitude and love of fashion-risk.

Ownership – the value of mistakes

Mistakes are great. Mistakes are brilliant – get on with making things happen, make mistakes and learn from them and try more stuff.

People make mistakes when you let them make decisions. They get a lot right too. Being as close as they are to where the action is, your team are absolutely the best people to be making more decisions for the business.

A few years back I went to New York to hear George Whalin – arguably America's best independent retail mind – speak. George has a lot to say about helping independent stores stand out from the multiples. What especially appeals to me about George's philosophy of nimble retailers adding value and creating customer delight, is that it is practical, real, proven and repeatable. It is scalable too; what works in one store will work in a hundred. Because it is scalable it was no surprise to discover that a number of senior people from the big chains were dotted around the large audience. I knew this because I'd earlier enjoyed a comic game of surreptitious delegate name-badge reading.

I spoke to a number of those directors and senior managers. A common theme emerged; they seemed to be there almost despite themselves. It was as if these people wanted to hear George speak just so they could then dismiss his thoughts as 'fine for the little guys but not realistic across my chain'. I asked them 'Do you think George's ideas work?' and a typical answer was: 'Yes, and he's got the numbers to prove it.' I went on to ask them why then could these ideas not work in their chain? A reply from a director of Petsmart sums up the responses: 'Our problem would be managing all this additional activity across our various channels and stores.' Wrong! That's your opportunity. Give your managers the scope to make things happen for themselves. Create local-promotion kits, train managers, give them budgets and a little freedom, and then let them go for it.

It is easy to see how senior central management can get scared about letting their store managers loose. But all the evidence tells us that this is wrong. Wherever proper decision-making power has been delegated down to individual store teams it has led to increased sales and profit. Yes it has also, sometimes, resulted in more mistakes being made. But mistakes are only unlearned lessons. You make one, you learn from it and you move on. Maybe that sounds a little too much like a homespun philosophy but it also happens to be true. Think about the early careers of people like Richard Branson, bankrupt in his teens, or Ray Krok the genius behind McDonalds who had a string of mistakes, false starts and lean-times behind him when, at 62, he spotted the potential for franchised fast food. Mistakes are made when you try something new, different or difficult. Sure you reduce your errors down to zero if you never try anything but just see what happens to your business when you do that.

Case study 5.4 *Not Smart Retail*: Where's the fire?

Before we move off respect, here's a cracking illustration that respect can still be a long way down the agenda at old-school retailers. In 2007 the 189-year-old Robbs department store in Hexham went into administration. Its 140 employees only learned of this after bosses set off the fire alarms to clear customers out and to gather staff together. When staff had gathered outside, they were told the bad news.

That's disrespectful, brutal and disgusting. The real tragedy here though is that as the company struggled on the year before, few of those 140 people were asked to help turn things around. Let's say the management pulled the same stunt a year earlier and instead of announcing closure used the opportunity to focus everyone's minds on the metaphorical fire threatening the business. A great leader would have had the guts to stand in front of those people and admit he/she needed their help. They would have formed fire-fighting teams to go through every aspect of the store looking for savings and for opportunities. That great leader would have taken the risk and empowered their people to get on and trade the store; the people of Hexham would have rallied to the cause too, I'm sure. I can't prove this in the Robbs case but I'm certain that asking for help in this way and getting everyone involved and empowered would have taken the business a damn sight closer to safety than the course they actually chose.

Respect people. Trust them. They'll often surprise you if you do.

Robbs' parent company was bought out and the store seems to be 'making a recovery, all that attention proved helpful after all.

Cornerstone three: recognition

Recognition is literally the habit of catching people doing good things and then saying 'thank you'. It is the single most powerful motivation tool business has ever been given. Motivated teams give better customer service, work happier together, are more efficient, more stable and they make life at work more enjoyable for all. That is because when you recognise an employee's contribution you send out a very strong message that says 'I'm glad you came to work today, you made a difference.' Recognition is the key component in motivation – we go into the other components in the next section but right now we're going to concentrate on the vital one.

Most people want to do the best job they can in any given situation. Recognition is the tool that tells them it has been worth making the effort. Recognition is self-reinforcing – people want to do a good job, you recognise them for it when they do, they feel good so they repeat the recognised action because they like feeling good. This may be a simplified representation of what actually goes on in our heads, but do you see how small moments of praise can escalate into improved performance?

Given that recognition is so powerful, why is it that retail managers are almost never trained in or assessed on their ability to do it effectively? I believe there are some simple reasons. The first is that recognition is hard to get right. Many of the moments that you will benefit from recognising and saying thank you for, are hard to measure. They might include such things as improving team spirit, giving exceptional customer service or going the extra mile. Recognition is less about direct sales numbers, although you will want to recognise contribution in that area too.

I suspect that it's the free nature of recognition that puts number-obsessed chain retailers off using it. This is a trust issue, and head offices are often not prepared to trust that store managers have the best view of the people around them. Recognition doesn't cost a penny and can drive store performance more effectively than almost any other management tool I have ever seen. You simply must use it.

Please don't make a fuss

One of the issues that makes recognition hard to do at first is a cultural one. The British are embarrassed by praise, we struggle to accept it. Indeed the most common response among British workers to receiving praise is to blush and to break eye contact. The strange parallel to that praise response is that we generally do not have the same problem when receiving criticism. When on the receiving end of criticism most British workers will listen, not always graciously, but they will listen. We all tend to have a system for receiving criticism, maybe not always a positive one but it is nonetheless a system. When it comes to receiving praise, although we really like the feeling, we are a little unsure of how to react.

There is also a crucial difference between the British delivery of praise and of criticism. We tend to be specific when criticising but only general when praising. I believe it is this lack of clarity that makes Brits so bad at giving and receiving praise. We give specific criticism such as 'the budget you did isn't right, where are the print costs?' whereas praise would be vague; 'nice work on the budget.' This is important because the whole point of praise and recognition is that we do it in such a way that recipients understand exactly what they did well so that they can repeat that behaviour. In the budget example above, the person who has been criticised knows they have to now go and sort out the print costs. The other person, praised with the 'nice work on the budget' comment, has no idea why this budget was better than the last one, or what it was exactly that they ought to repeat to get some more praise next time. Better praise would have been 'I like how you've laid out the budget, that's going to make it easier for me to get it approved. Thanks.'

'Doing' recognition

'Little and often' is a brilliant management maxim. It's absolutely perfect when applied to recognition. To make too much of a moment of praise can make everybody feel uncomfortable. It can even sometimes encourage resentment from the team towards whoever you have singled out for extra-double helpings of praise. You are not attempting to make an individual feel like they are God's gift to retail. If the thing they've done is really special then by all means mention it at a team meeting. Spot something good, mention it quickly, say 'thank you', be specific.

The bad recognition habits we managers get into, often because we're embarrassed by praise, include: worrying about singling out individuals, delaying praise, overblowing praise, concentrating on catching people getting it wrong and not being specific with our praise. Delaying praise reduces the effectiveness of recognition. Recognition works best when fresh.

Too many people build their management style around spotting staff making mistakes and then correcting the errors. If you are one of them, try catching people doing good things instead. Do that and you will quickly find that staff actively attempt to repeat those good things and that they look for more and more good things to do. Recognition taps into so many crucial psychological needs. The easy bit to accept is that recognition, done properly, makes people feel good.

Recognition taps into so many crucial psychological needs.

It is also nice to sometimes link recognition to small rewards but this actually isn't at all critical. Study after study shows that the part employees actually value is that moment where their manager, or a colleague, or a customer, says 'thank you for ...'

Behaviours

Although a good recognition habit is all about being spontaneous and saying 'thank you' whenever you see the need, it helps to have in mind a list of the sorts of things that you will be looking out to give praise for. At the risk of sounding like I've been snacking on a jargon butty, what you should be basing your recognition on are 'observable positive behaviours'. Essentially that's all the good stuff people do that you can spot them doing.

When you first decide to introduce recognition, putting together a list of these 'observable positive behaviours' helps the whole team to get a handle on what it is that you are looking for. Once you've sat down and really thought about these behaviours you can stick a list up on the noticeboard. Give a copy to new starters and use it as a basis for review meetings.

'Observable' is the key word in this bit of jargon. It tells you that the behaviours you are looking for are those that you actually have to 'see' happen. Sales is not an 'observable positive behaviour' because it is an activity that a) you already measure closely in the performance numbers, and b) you will be discussing the sales action with each member of the team anyway.

What would be an 'observable positive behaviour' is when you spot someone going out of their way to make a customer happy. With any luck that behaviour will show up as a sale too, but even if it doesn't that customer has left the store with a good feeling about your business. That is worth its weight in gold but in a way that is very hard to see from just looking at the hard performance numbers.

Take a look at pages 98–105 for a little set of illustrations of observable positive behaviours in action.

Easy ways to 'do' recognition

There are two easy routes you can go down to build specific recognition into your team culture. Doing specific recognition needs to be learned so don't be embarrassed that it might not be part of your current style. You will get there by practise. Equally don't assume that because you do often say 'thank you' that you are getting recognition right. I'll lay down good money that, if you are honest with yourself, you will find that 90 per cent of those 'thank you' moments are non-specific.

In the four years between the first edition and the one you're reading now, loads of managers have fed back that this part of the book is the one they were most sceptical about, but that once they'd done it was the most rewarding. I guess I'm asking you to disconnect the cynicism for a bit and give this stuff a go.

Method one – the 20-second ceremony

Use a couple of team meetings to make up your team's list of 'observable positive behaviours'. A good way to get a great list together is to start with the mission statement and values and think about the kind of things you can do to support them.

Now make up some 'thank you' notes. These should have space on them for the recipient's name and a bigger space for you to write down why you are pleased enough to want to say 'thank you'. Print out a bunch of these and keep some in your pocket at all times. Whenever you see an opportunity to say 'thank you', fill one out quickly and go put it into the hand of the person you want to say 'thanks' to. You don't even have to say 'thanks' out loud if you don't feel you can. You don't have to make a song and dance of it. You don't even have to speak if you feel uncomfortable. What is important is that the exchange of this note is something both of you understand: it tells the recipient that you have noticed and that you are pleased, nothing more, nothing less.

Dish out blank 'thank you' notes to the team too. Encourage everyone to use these 'thank you' notes. Workmates recognising each other's efforts has almost as much power as when you do it. You have really cracked it when you get customers to fill in 'thank you' notes too.

The 20-second ceremony works so well. It is unobtrusive too. I've seen this work successfully in a mad-busy tiny KFC that was processing 50,000 lunch transactions a week. People really do respond to it. The notes can feel a bit silly at first but that soon goes and the process of recognition becomes part of the everyday team culture. You will never find a cheaper or more effective way in which to transform your team's performance.

Method two – the heroes board

Allocate a piece of wall space to recognition. Make up some 'thank you' notes similar to the ones mentioned above. Start giving them to people under the same criteria, and tell recipients to bang them up on the wall. This method introduces a little bit of peer-pressure because everyone can see who is being praised, but you might find it more comfortable for you than recognition method one.

In both methods you can use the best examples to determine what you do with your non-cash rewards (which we go through in Chapter 6). It's quite nice to build in a little focus at team meetings for recognition. It's even more effective to use one such meeting, each week, for a little bit of extra recognition. Take the best 'thank you' or 'hero' example from that week and give the person a decent bottle of wine, a case of beer, flowers or good chocolates. Not too much – just so it feels great to receive and it really sets the scene for a rousing and effective team meeting.

Case study 5.5 *Smart Retail*: KFC and the 20-second recognition ceremony

KFC transformed their company in the UK in the late 1990s and have strengthened their position ever since. It is a fantastic retail fast-food business. One of the major transformation focuses was on the way in which they treated their people. As part of that process they introduced a recognition programme based on observable positive behaviours and on the 20-second recognition ceremony.

A beautiful example of how this tiny, simple ceremony could affect the way people felt about themselves and their performance came to me at a post-launch regional meeting. A manager, Mike, told me what had happened when he went through the 20-second ceremony for the first time. In fact he told me he'd made somebody cry doing it, so I thought we might be in trouble. Dawn had worked at her KFC outlet for nearly 10 years. She had seen managers come and go but had never been keen to take on that sort of extra responsibility for herself. She liked being one of the team and that was that. Mike had been her manager for nearly six months.

One morning Mike spotted Dawn showing a new member of staff how to 'double bag' a waste bin. Double bagging means putting in two bin-liners at a time so that at lunch, when the bin is full, you only have to throw one bag of waste away and the bin already has its next liner in place. Now this is a tiny thing, saving maybe a minute at peak time. But Mike saw Dawn do this and it occurred to him that he had seen Dawn help new people learn the ropes on countless occasions. She didn't have to, it wasn't part of her job, she just liked to do it. So Mike decided to use one of his 'thank you' notes. He wrote it out and ticked a box that said 'For making new members of the team feel welcome' and, in his own words, he 'shyly handed it to Dawn'.

Dawn burst into tears, Mike reassured her that it wasn't a P45 he'd just given her and asked what the matter was. So she told him 'You've never said "thank you" to me before.' Mike became quite indignant and replied that he had, often, at shift meetings. Dawn put him right: 'No, you've said "thanks" to the team at those times, and that's nice but you've never come to me, looked me in the eye and made it so clear that something good I do has been noticed. And actually none of my managers over the years has either.'

Dawn felt great about that moment of recognition, that's why there were tears. So do most people. What's so nice about this approach is that its effect snowballs. Slowly but surely, more people begin to repeat the good things they do more often, and that gently spreads throughout the business.

6

CHAPTER SIX

How to get people out of bed

Motivated staff are critical to the success of your store. Hopefully you will have already read the previous chapter on store cultures. If you have then you are already on the way to enjoying the benefits of having a motivated team around you. In this section we're going to get a bit deeper into the nitty gritty of motivation. In particular I'd like to suggest some practical moves you can make to improve the motivation of your team.

If you're going to build a great culture in your store, a motivated team is essential. Just to recap, the benefits of a great store culture include cost savings, customer service quality improvements, people pulling together to deliver the company values, better support for your decisions and a more enjoyable time at work.

The components of motivation

Individuals are motivated by a combination of:

▶ Financial reward

▶ Implied sanction

▶ Self-respect

▶ Non-financial reward

▶ Recognition of value contributed.

Of course the impact of each motivating component will be different for different people. Factors such as age, personal circumstances and social considerations all have an impact. Most of these make for only really subtle changes in your approach though, with one exception. The younger members of your team are often disproportionately motivated by cash.

Financial reward   Show me the money

The most common mistake we all make on motivation is to assume that financial rewards are the most important and most motivating thing we can offer. The truth is – and this might be hard to accept because it is counter-intuitive – that money has very little motivating effect beyond a certain point. So long as the wage is fair anything over that, such as special bonuses or massive cash competitions, has very little additional impact on employee motivation. People love getting it, sure, but it can even be counterproductive because the payment of large bonuses tends to condition staff to only ever put in extra effort if they can see a wad of cash in it for themselves. Pay too little, however, and money becomes an astonishingly important demotivator.

Those retailers with the most motivated workforces have observed that offering significant cash rewards in exchange for performance improvements has three effects:

1   It drives too much focus into short-term revenue generation at the cost of falls in customer service quality.

2   It conditions employees to only go beyond the job description when they are offered a cash incentive to do so.

3   Bonuses become absorbed quickly into the employees' general budgets and as such are not remembered over the longer term.

There is a whole filing cabinet full of research that suggests that cash triggers only very short-term satisfaction in the mind of the recipient. It boils down to cash being, by its nature, ephemeral – here today and gone tomorrow. I know you probably still don't believe me but this effect has been observed time and time again. Money is important but it doesn't create long-term motivation. You might need to trust me on this one.

Money is important but it doesn't create long-term motivation.

Incidentally you can measure employee motivation by looking at factors such as employee satisfaction, employee turnover rates and customer service quality scores.

Implied sanction   The stick to your carrot

Implied sanction is the stick to your reward-carrot. It is the rulebook. It's 'implied' because you may never have to use it but the team knows you would if pressed. It's 'sanction' because it's what happens when the list of minimum standards is not met. Implied sanction is a strong motivating factor but one that requires significant skill to manage effectively. It takes a lot of common sense too, and certainly sympathy with the concept of 'treat others the way you would like them to treat you'.

A sales assistant, for example, needs to know that a drop in customer satisfaction will lead to a serious chat. Further they must know that the serious chat will generate a set of actions that, if not carried out, will cast serious doubt over their future in the store. That's the sanction part.

The team needs to know that sanction is possible but at the same time they must not be working in paralysed fear of that sanction. It's a tricky balancing act sometimes but much better than the alternative, which is to manage by fear. Management by fear generates lots of problems such as decreases in service quality. Frightened staff don't work well with customers. Fear can also lead to increased employee turnover and even industrial disputes.

In the 1980s hard-bastard macho managers dominated retail management. Fear was a powerful motivator then because unemployment hung over pretty much everyone all of the time. Times have changed; there have been retail vacancies going unfilled in the UK for some years now. Management by fear is a poor technique but we must recognise that we're all human. A lack of sanction for those times when we let standards slip lets us become lazy. To motivate you must ensure that the team knows you have set standards for a good reason and that you will maintain them vigorously.

Successful one-to-ones

When you have to actually use sanction be quick, be clear and be fair. Here's the best format for a one-to-one in which you have to discipline a member of your team.

▶ 10 minutes to explain the general principles of the situation.

▶ 5 minutes to very specifically discuss the weakness or failure of the individual.

▶ 15 minutes to then explain why you have faith in that person's ability to turn the situation around. This is the time to rebuild that person's belief in themselves and their abilities. Make sure you finish the meeting with the person feeling on a high.

You can probably see a lot of the *1-Minute Manager* in that process and that's fine. This is the practical way for retailers to do the same thing. Over the years a number of store managers have recommended variations on this method to me, but I'd like to specifically credit Umesh Vadodaria of PC World for this version.

Self-respect Treat me like a grown up

We looked at respect in the earlier section on store culture. I go into it at a more practical level here and concentrate on building self-respect in individual members of your team.

The default position for the majority of British workers is to do the best job we can. If you create the right conditions most people will work hard to deliver a good result. What stands behind that reality is self-respect. I've already looked at how the best teams are built on respect, and self-respect is the crucial component of that. It's what makes people feel it's worth making the effort.

The opposite is also true: put individuals into situations where they are robbed of their self-respect and they will react accordingly. People will steal and treat customers with contempt – and why not? If you take away somebody's self-respect how can you ever expect that person to in turn respect your customers?

Without wishing to get horribly political, I'd like to ask you to take a look at what poverty and unemployment do to communities. Take away a person's job, put them in a cheap house they don't own or ever could, and crime, drugs and malcontent flourish. The truth is that if I don't respect myself I'm not going to respect you. You can do such a lot as a store manager to encourage self-respect to grow among the members of your team.

Share information

Tell the team the confidential stuff: state of the cash flow, company health, costs, losses and profits. Show that you trust them with such sensitive numbers. Yes, some of it will find its way to your competitors but the losses will be vastly outweighed by the benefits.

Delegate power

Allow team members to make decisions for themselves, especially on discounts and customer service issues. Give people the confidence to make these decisions by ensuring that you have a good set of practical and sensible guidelines in place. Good procedures help people to make good decisions.

Delegate responsibility

Make members of the team responsible for the performance of specific departments. Responsibility is a powerful source of self-respect, especially when combined with a variable such as profitability or sales revenue.

Encourage training

Make sure everyone who wants it has access to all of the training opportunities available. Make a habit of promoting manufacturer-sponsored training and seminars too. These are often of a high quality and they make a welcome break from the usual company formats. You are saying to the team members who go on these courses 'I value you and I want to give you access to skills you'll find useful.'

Share the good jobs

Make members of the team responsible for specific tasks, especially those 'cushy' jobs managers sometimes keep for themselves.

Muck in

If you expect the team to polish and dust, do it yourself too and show that it is not a job that's 'beneath you'.

Listen to both sides

When a customer complains, listen to both sides of the issue. Don't blame the salesperson in front of the customer; you are responsible for service quality so you make the apology. Then go talk with the salesperson and if there really is an issue give them an opportunity to suggest ways in which to solve it.

Don't wash your dirty linen in public

Never embarrass or dress-down a colleague in public. I once observed some bully of a supermarket manager having a go at a cleaner in front of customers. This cleaner had been skiving but that didn't matter, the manager ended up looking like a nasty piece of work. That reflected badly on the shop.

Consider the rulebook

Is there anything really daft in the rulebook that just forces people to do stupid things? If there is then get rid of it.

Let others do the talking

Give everybody who wants a chance to run team meetings. Encourage staff to present ideas at these meetings too. Go with the three-slide rule to prevent meetings becoming too competitive or boring: one to set-up the 'what it is', one to explain 'how it is' and a final slide to summarise 'why it is.'

Listen

Shut up and listen to what people are telling you before you go making up your mind. Ask questions and allow people to give you the whole story. People respond better when they feel like they are being listened to.

Encourage every opportunity for feedback

Get and give feedback on ideas, interviews, worries, suggestions and concerns. Do this in an honest, active way. Take things on board. If the answer to an idea or issue is 'yes', then get on and do it. If the answer is 'don't know', go find out what you need to know. If the answer is 'no', explain why. Offering a shrug and a 'because it just is' is never acceptable. Always do these things within a short timeframe.

Build people back up

If you ever have to pull somebody up, discipline them or criticise their performance then always build that person back up again afterwards. Leave people on a high.

Don't bad mouth people

Every time you say 'so and so is an idiot' in front of your team you send a negative message about your attitude to colleagues. Negative talk infects your team – just don't do it!

Negative talk infects your team – just don't do it!

Recognise contribution

Learn to give specific praise as well as specific criticism. This is really very hard to do at first but is the most powerful motivating force of them all. Recognition is free and makes a real difference. By giving recognition you are giving person X a reason to feel that getting out of bed and coming to work today was worth it. The key to recognition is to be specific, to do it as soon as you think about it, and to do it little and often.

Celebrate success

Absolutely essential to the strength of the team is making time, and plenty of it, to celebrate success. I don't mean the embarrassing forced stuff such as ringing a bell every time somebody makes a sale though. Celebrating success means saying 'well done' to people. It means making a small fuss of good things in the daily team meetings. It means going off for a pizza and a beer together. Toasting a hard-won target feels great. It feels even better if you've talked one of your suppliers into paying for the beer.

People need to know that the effort they've put into achieving something had a point to it. Celebrating success is one critical way in which you can do that. It says 'I'm proud of us, we took on a challenge and we beat it together'. I cannot stress enough that you will gain many times over from putting aside a proper budget for doing this.

Be ready to admit your own mistakes

If you get it wrong be honest about it and move on: 'Okay I got this wrong, now how can you help me to do this right next time?'

Put the customer at the centre

Show your people that you respect them by showing them that you're all working together for the same boss: the customer. It is the customer that we really work for. They are the ones who pay our wages. Teams need to have focus and in retail the customer is the best target for that focus. Everything you do must be built around the notion of helping customers leave the store with a smile on their face.

Using non-financial rewards Let's have a laugh now

'Non-financial rewards' is just a name for the fun stuff. They can include all sorts of things such as extra days off, flash cars for a month, gift vouchers, freebies and holidays. Now there is a really, really fine line here between exciting and tacky. It's so easy to make rewards embarrassing. Worse, lots of retailers go for the big dramatic holiday-type incentives where only one person can win anything significant. Maybe the best performing store manager gets to go to Bermuda for a fortnight. I've often worked with clients, employing thousands of people, who have insisted on running these demotivating incentive structures. They launch huge incentive programmes worth big money but concentrated into maybe five prizes only. Fantastic for the lucky five – but actually all this succeeds in doing is turning off the thousands who are pretty sure they won't win. Worse, out of the 200 who think they are in with a chance, 195 high-achievers are left feeling positively demotivated when they don't win that holiday.

When it comes to all motivating rewards, including cash bonuses, recognition and non-cash bonuses, little and often is best. In this case 'little' because that means you can spread the budget much further and in doing so touch many more people. 'Often' because it keeps things fresh and gives you lots of opportunities to boost performance without programmes going stale.

It's how you use the little non-financial rewards that's critical. As either an owner of an independent or as a chain-store manager you have lots of freedom to do what you think will work best. Buddy up with the manufacturer's reps. Let them do some training at your store one evening and suggest they give the expense account a workout by taking the team for a curry afterwards. I'm always pleasantly pleased by how consistent manufacturer's reps are in this regard. They always say 'yes' eventually.

As a store-owner you should be doing these things anyway, out of your own pocket. Incidentally, building in an ideas session before you eat is a good way of recouping the cost. I believe too that running a little meeting like this before noshing down has a positive effect on how you later have to account for the expense tax-wise, but don't quote me on that.

The wrong way to use non-cash rewards is to over-hype the reward or to use inappropriate rewards. So, for example, offering to give someone a CD for doing 200 per cent of their target is an insult to you both. It would be wrong too to make a shy person stand on a chair to receive a commemorative 'Top Guy' plaque. Use your best judgement and knowledge of the individual: what works for one might well turn off another.

Buy the team a daft gift each at Christmas but hand-write a thank you note on each package. It reminds people that they are important to you.

Always generously mark people's birthdays, weddings and new babies. Preferably do so out of your own pocket rather than via a staff whipround.

Try to include your employees' partners on social invites. Partners have a massive influence on your people and on their view of you. A career in retail entails strange and challenging hours that take people away from their families. Don't make that worse by extending this exclusion to the team's social occasions. Getting partners involved in idea generation can be very effective too.

Picture: Koworld

Shopping is fun, we should all remember that.

Great non-cash incentives produced out of almost nothing

A good tip is to save any freebies you receive as a manager and pass them on to the team rather than keep them for yourself. Some managers save up these goodies and freebies to use in one go. Others dish them out straight away. Either way you must ensure that you don't fall into either of these traps:

1   Only ever giving stuff to the loudest members of the team because they are the ones you notice.
2   Showing favouritism to a person who the team could, conceivably, suspect you of having more than a professional interest in.

Here are two ways of avoiding these freebie pitfalls and at the same time bringing some fun to the proceedings.

Team ballot

Say you've been lucky enough to find yourself with four bottles of champagne, two boxes of Belgian chocolates and a stack of good promotional T-shirts. It happens! Over a week you have the team agree to nominate a colleague each for a thank you. All they have to do is write down the other person's name and a line on why they should be thanked. The key to participation is that anyone who doesn't make a nomination is disqualified from winning a prize themselves.

Then you all pile down the pub after close-of-play one evening. Get a round in and read out the 'thank you' notes. Everyone who has been nominated gets to choose a random envelope. Try to make sure that everyone who should have been has been nominated. Inside each envelope is a note telling them which of the freebies they've earned.

This is effective because the team sees that you could have held onto all the stuff yourself but preferred them to have it. People love that – they really do. Asking them to self-select worthy recipients gets people focused on their place in the team too. Team ballots are not heavy affairs but they really do work. Aim to run one every six months or every quarter at a push.

Balloon day

This method of giving away all your freebies can be hilarious, great fun, nicely competitive and very motivating. On one of your busiest days you fill your office with balloons. Each balloon contains confetti and a little envelope that has the name of a prize in it. To spice things up a little, I usually chuck in some envelopes with fivers in them and some with a token for something silly like a choccy bar. Then you draw up a big chart with the names of all your team on it.

Now you need to set a challenge. Challenges can include such things as:

▶ Sell a specific item.

▶ Gain an 'excellent' score on a customer service questionnaire (do this as an exit survey; have someone stand on the door with a clipboard gathering answers).

▶ Selling add-ons; score a point for every transaction that includes a legitimate add-on (legitimate meaning the add-on was actually something that the customer will have been glad to have been sold).

Each time a person completes a unit of the challenge they earn a 'pop'.

You can also award random 'free pops' to members of the team, especially to anyone who isn't actively involved in selling. Do this whenever you observe a positive behaviour. Those positive behaviours could include such things as solving a customer complaint or helping out a colleague. Each time a person earns a 'pop' they get a token. These tokens are sticky and you can encourage people to stick them on the chart as the day goes on.

At the end of the day, after the punters have gone home, everyone gathers outside your office. Maybe you open some refreshments to help get the team revved up for the popping to commence. Starting with the person who has earned most 'pops' you let each person into the room to pop the number of balloons they've earned during the day. Then they get to keep whatever falls out of the balloons.

I've run this one many times and it always gets everybody going. It's nice if you can make the balloon day coincide with a team night out afterwards too. There are lots of variations on this theme such as having the prizes in lockers or in a sandbox and so on. I'm sure you can think up some yourselves too.

Recognition and motivation

Each of the motivating factors we've gone through here does in itself also have a recognition component. Giving out prizes is recognition, trusting somebody to make decisions is recognition and bonuses are also a form of recognition. In case you've missed it, refer to the recognition part of Chapter 5 for loads more on how to use recognition to motivate.

Team meetings

You'll have seen above how important communication, team-building, recognition, respect and trust are. One of the most useful opportunities to make things happen in these areas is your daily team meeting.

Yeah, I said 'daily' team meeting.

I recommend you hold a 5 to 15 minute team meeting every single day. You don't have to do this but all the best retailers do. It's hard to build a team spirit if the team never gets to stop and spend a few minutes focusing together. Equally, what better way is there to swap ideas, to jump onto opportunities and to share responsibilities?

Daily team meetings are the missing ingredient in many otherwise great store managers' repertoires.

Daily team meetings are the missing ingredient in many otherwise great store managers' repertoires. Grab your store diary now and write five headings into tomorrow's date and run a meeting around those five things. Some of the items worth covering in team meetings include:

▶ Customer service issues and how these were solved

▶ Forthcoming events

▶ Promotions

▶ New products just in

- ▶ Bargains identified
- ▶ Review competitor activity
- ▶ Review new best practice ideas identified
- ▶ Discuss incentive schemes
- ▶ Review any challenges
- ▶ Introduce new employees
- ▶ Review targets and performance
- ▶ Celebrate success
- ▶ Recognition
- ▶ Consider improvement ideas

Even if you can only do the last one, it will have been worth having the meeting. The next chapter talks you through how to find loads of these …

CHAPTER SEVEN

All we need is a little better every time

Ideas are the fuel for organisations. What you do with those ideas, how you convert them into action and improvements, is what then makes the organisation grow and prosper. Space for improvement can be readily found in all areas, especially in technique, systems, presentation, recruitment and performance. All retailers can benefit from a culture of everyday performance improvement but few try to. Don Taylor and Jeanne Smalling-Archer, authors of the very helpful *Up Against the Wal-Marts* call this kaizen, as does Julian Richer in his awesome book *The Richer Way*. Others use different names for the same thing. Kaizen is Japanese for 'continuous improvement involving everyone'.

I don't think we need to slap a Japanese jargon word onto the making of improvements. For me the task is as simple, and as vital, as 'let's do it a little better every time'. That sets up a very simple question for your team members: 'How could I do this again, only better?' Your mission statement comes in here because it helps define what 'better' means. At TNT, whose mission used to be 'to deliver every parcel on time', 'better' would mean faster, safer, or cheaper. For retailers, 'better' will usually mean faster, cheaper but still better for the customer.

Improvement in this sense isn't necessarily about massive earth-shattering changes. What we are looking for are those everyday improvements. Improvements in the ways in which we look after each other, our relationships with customers and the quality and relevance of our processes. A typical example might be the discovery that one piece of paperwork can be integrated with some other process rather than be dealt with separately. Combining the two will save money and time, so that's an improvement. It could be the realisation that the rules of a promotion we've created can be simplified to the benefit of the customer, and that is an improvement too.

Gathering improvement ideas

You will need to have two things in place:

1　A way to gather ideas.

2　An improvements slot on the agenda for discussion at team meetings.

If you were to look at just one task or process in each daily team meeting you will have seven improvements each week, 30 for the month and 365 over a year. That's awesome. Okay, so maybe you won't get into this every day but you will still generate a significant store of improvement ideas every month. Working in this way is easy. You are not attempting to change the world in a day, you are just looking to change one little thing at a time. Every journey starts with just a single step – remember that.

Every journey starts with just a single step – remember that.

Do you currently change anything each month? Does change only ever happen dramatically once a year? 'Let's do it a little better every time' puts you in the driving seat of change. Your team becomes a valuable engine of change.

Statisticians are blind – the measurement trap

Plenty of otherwise sensible people believe that you cannot improve that which you cannot measure. That's dangerous, wrong even, and here's why: some of the most effective tools to improve customer satisfaction are unmeasurable in a conventional sense. Smiling at a customer – warm genuine smiles, not the fixed leer of the street nutter – has proved to be one of the most effective ways to make customers feel better about you and your company. How do you measure the number of smiles your team gives out?

Here's something to think about: a number of aspects of sexual performance can be measured. Factors such as duration, the dimensions of various body parts, room temperature, heartbeats/minute can all be easily recorded and measured (you might need somebody with a clipboard to come in and write this stuff down for you though). But do any of these factors automatically add up to guaranteed great sex? Of course not.

Measuring the wrong things is a real trap. This is a grim example but it's worth telling. A US Army General noticed that the daily success of the Vietnam War was being measured by relative casualty rates. A measure as crude and unpleasant as 'if we kill more of them than they do us then we must be winning'. Convinced this measure did not convey a useful picture, this General instead created a set of metrics that also took into account territory, specific objectives and economic cost.

It is what the General said about his reasons for doing this that is absolutely relevant to retailing. He said 'we are only making important that which we can easily measure, when actually we should be measuring only that which is important.' For example, just because you can measure unit sales easily, that does not make it the most important part of your business to concentrate your improvement efforts in. Customer satisfaction is harder to measure but far more important because it relates to unit sales made today, tomorrow and next year.

Case study 7.1 *Not Smart Retail*: The classic measurement mistake

In the early 1980s the Coca-Cola Company had become incredibly twitchy about the strengthening performance of Pepsi, their nearest rival. Pepsi had made big strides into Coke's market and one stat in particular had the executives at Coke sweating: in 1972, 18 per cent of drinkers said they drank Coke exclusively against just 4 per cent choosing Pepsi. By the start of the '80s this ratio had moved to 12 per cent favouring Coke exclusively and 11 per cent Pepsi.

And that's when Pepsi made its genius move and unleashed 'The Pepsi Challenge'. Pepsi targeted committed Coke drinkers and presented them with two small cups of cola, one marked 'Q' and one marked 'M'. Almost without fail drinkers would take a sip and choose 'M' – which would of course then be revealed as Pepsi.

Initially the team at Coke attempted to claim that Pepsi's campaign was fixed. But when they then ran similar experiments themselves they discovered a 53 per cent to 47 per cent split in favour of Pepsi. For the market leader this was a bombshell – the impact of a six percentage point spread could be measured in millions of dollars in potential lost revenue.

The team were horrified and commissioned a slew of additional market research projects. Each came back with similar results and attempts to qualify the choice for Pepsi began to suggest that Americans had fallen out of love with Coke's distinct 'bite'. What was once described as 'refreshing' became 'harsh'; the same tasters began to associate words like 'smooth' and 'rounded' with Pepsi and went on to suggest they preferred these attributes.

Roy Stout was the head of Coke's consumer marketing research team and is the man who made the connection between losing market share and product taste. He reasoned: *'If we have twice as many vending machines, have more shelf space, spend more on advertising and are competitively priced, why are we losing [market share]? You look at the Pepsi Challenge and you have to begin asking about taste.'*[1]

This bombshell drove the board at Coke to make an extraordinary decision – they would change the hitherto sacred and world-famous secret Coke recipe to take account of the perceived change in America's cola preferences. And thus was born 'New Coke', which had a lighter and sweeter taste, a taste more like Pepsi in fact.

Early test results were good – New Coke pulled level with Pepsi on blind tasting preferences. A little more tinkering followed and New Coke began to pull out a persistent six to eight per cent lead. The board then took the decision to take it to market and launched a massive campaign behind the new formula.

All the research said New Coke would be a winner.

It failed and failed dramatically. Tens of thousands of Coke drinkers rose up in protest, sales of the new drink faltered and, cutting a long story short, the company was forced into a humiliating climb down and reintroduced the original formula as Classic Coke. Very shortly afterwards sales of New Coke all but evaporated. Why?

The flaw was, in hindsight, a very simple one. Coke has a predominantly citrusy-burst flavour where Pepsi has a more raisiny-vanilla taste. Take one or two sips of Coke and the experience is quite sharp, the bite is very strong. Do the same with a can of Pepsi and the first gulps are much smoother, sweeter and gentle on the palate.

But ... drink a whole can of either cola and the experience changes completely. And this is the flaw – Coke drinkers like the way a can of Coke tastes but they don't entirely like the first few sips. Coke drinkers who prefer the first sips of Pepsi when tested blind, often complain of a cloying sweetness when they then go on to drink the whole can.

New Coke is a fantastic example of an entire company both putting too much emphasis on the research and on ignoring instinct and emotion. So what were the real reasons for Coke's slipping market share?

Consensus of opinion is that Coke had allowed their marketing spend to mature along with their product. They had failed to sell to the younger, hipper, cola drinkers that Pepsi had become so adept at communicating with. Coke's customers were leaching away to a preference for coffee, and later bottled waters, whereas Pepsi's were still enjoying rotting their teeth on 'The Choice of a New Generation'.

I'm not entirely discrediting management by numbers but stories like this one go a long way to proving that without the emotional context you don't have the full story.

[1] Stats and background information taken from *Blink* by Malcolm Gladwell (Penguin, 2006), an essential read for retailers.

Go with your gut feel

Use your gut feel and allow yourself to apply improvements even to those processes, tasks and interactions to which you are unable to attach numbers. I'd like to ask you to consider valuing the power of your gut feel more highly. Gut feel isn't random. It's a guide, an instinct that tells you a certain path may be the right one to take. It is also that good sense which tells you not to do something. But it needs tuning: books like this one exist to help you separate out correct gut feel judgements from other emotional factors such as fear or laziness.

Even science is now beginning to come round to seeing gut feel as something real and valuable. There is a credible theory that suggests decisions made on gut feel are more often than not the carefully calculated result of our experience and knowledge, and that instinctive gut feel decisions get better as we add new experiences and knowledge to our memories. Think of your gut feel as a potent business weapon, a weapon that is unique to you.

Think of your gut feel as a potent business weapon, a weapon that is unique to you.

I wish I had more space here to go into instinct and gut feel in greater detail but you want to read more about shops and that. Luckily there are already two brilliant books out there you can read instead: *Blink* by Malcolm Gladwell (Penguin, 2006) is really good at explaining the process at work in instinct-led decision making – *See Feel Think Do* by Andy Milligan and Shaun Smith (Cyan, 2006) is even better at helping you to build your confidence in using gut instinct to make decisions. If you only fancy reading one get Andy and Shaun's – it's really very, very good and you'll get a lot from it.

Making improvement work for you

Let's do it a little better every time. As well as running through ideas to apply this principle to at team meetings, you will need to create an environment in which the team feels comfortable to try things and to suggest things. If you are the kind of person who greets every new idea with 'I'd love to change that but ...' or 'I can't see that working' then soon people will stop trying and suggesting. Equally if members of the team feel that you are likely to discipline them for making mistakes then no one is going to want to try anything new for fear of punishment.

Get the culture of improvement established. Allow your people to question how they do things and you will benefit enormously. Make that an everyday occurrence – little steps but lots of them – and you and your customers will feel those improvements take hold.

Room for improvement

The best retailers do not stand still when successful. They strive to keep the momentum, to keep growing and to keep moving forward. That growth and movement is inspired by tiny little everyday improvements just as much as it is by sweeping change.

Here are some of the categories in which you will always be able to find lots of opportunities to improve things. The thoughts listed here are a deliberate mix of actual ideas and of pointers to get you looking in the right places for ideas of your own.

You might like to pick out a single line during daily team meetings and have the team come up with some thoughts and ideas on that theme.

Improvement and customers

▶ Consider everything from the customer's perspective.

▶ Encourage customers to tell you their complaints.

▶ Listen to them sincerely when they do.

▶ Think about the type of people who come into your shop.

▶ Make changes that bring people to you who currently shop with your competitors.

▶ Talk to customers all the time.

▶ Aim to improve average transaction values.

▶ Use eye contact.

▶ Walk your store like a customer would.

▶ If you can get hold of former customers ask them why they don't love you anymore.

▶ Whenever you are resolving a customer complaint ask customers how they would improve your service.

▶ Remember names.

▶ Think carefully about the integrity of your pricing.

▶ Send them stuff they might actually like to see.

▶ Where can you add value to the customer experience?

▶ What can you promise today that is better than yesterday?

▶ Run surveys.

▶ List the benefits of doing business with you and then tell customers about them.

▶ What do other people do well that you really ought to be ripping off for yourselves?

▶ List all the things in your store that regularly delight customers – then think about how to double the list.

▶ Are you leading by example?

▶ Write down a list of all the processes that touch customers directly – all of them.

▶ Then do a list of all those that don't – can you strip any of these out?

▶ Make it easy for customers to feed back to you – use suggestion boxes, till receipt surveys, telephone aftercare calls, open evenings and everything else you can think of.

▶ Get customer opinion on new products before you put those products into your range.

▶ Ask customers to tell you what's missing.

▶ Ask customers to tell you what they like about your store.

Improvement and you

▶ Read stuff.

▶ Get involved in the business community – join your street or shopping centre advisory committee or the chamber of commerce.

▶ Ask people about your management style.

▶ Learn from those below you as well as above you.

▶ Seek out examples of great retailers and learn from them.

▶ Sign up to every Internet resource you can find – here's three corkers for a start: www.theretailbulletin.com, www.nrf.com and www.george-whalin.com

▶ What things do you do outside work that might be useful inside?

▶ Make an honest list of your strengths.

▶ Then one of your weaknesses.

▶ Go on courses.

▶ Sign up to every training and seminar resource you can initially – the more you go on the better you will become at recognising which ones are going to be truly useful in future.

▶ As naff as it might seem, set life goals and then yearly goals for yourself – what do these goals tell you about the areas in which you will need to concentrate personal improvements?

▶ Listen to people more than talk to people.

▶ Open your eyes!

▶ Go shopping more often – do things your customers do.

▶ Read the trade press.

▶ Learn from competitors.

▶ Learn from people outside your sector.

▶ Maintain your standards.

▶ Appoint an honest and strong assistant manager – who will soon let you know where you have room for improvement.

▶ Improve the balance of your life: you look after shops – shopping is fun. Try to see it more that way.

Improvement and colleagues

▶ Reward people for improving things.

▶ Consider issues from your team's perspective.

▶ Don't get mad with people for trying.

▶ Let grown-ups think for themselves – empower people to make their own improvements.

▶ Encourage talk, talk and more talk – leave every feedback channel open all the time.

▶ Give people a look at the lists on these pages.

▶ Buy employees a copy of *Smart Retail* for Christmas – remember to wrap it up nice. In fact, get your Mum a copy too, and all your friends.

▶ Recognise people's contributions.

▶ Don't rip off your staff.

▶ Never criticise employees in front of anyone else.

▶ Build a great culture founded on trust and respect.

▶ Tell people you are chuffed with them whenever they make you feel that way.

▶ Are your job descriptions a jargon-filled sack of nonsense?

▶ Feel free to build friendships but never forget that you are the boss – keep a perspective.

▶ Encourage the team to be open about mistakes.

▶ Have a laugh together.

▶ Always, always celebrate success.

▶ Be human in your relationships – if someone is going through a life crisis help them cope with it.

▶ Share the numbers – let the team own them as much as you do.

▶ Pay a profit-related bonus.

▶ Pay a customer service-related bonus.

▶ Smile when you walk through the door every morning even if you don't feel like it.

▶ Make sure everyone knows about all available courses and seminars.

▶ Put aside cash for training.

▶ Let good people go on courses you've been on – use training as a reward.

▶ Be specific with instructions.

▶ Sales assistants get closest to your customers – listen to what they tell you about those customers.

▶ Challenge people and encourage them to challenge themselves.

▶ Teach by example.

▶ Show people that the best way to do things is to consider solutions rather than dwell on problems.

▶ Get the team involved in all the big decisions.

▶ Help employees to see that it is customers, not you, who pay their wages.

▶ Hold regular one-to-one appraisals but be prepared to allow employees to tell you what they think of you, of your business and of the team too.

▶ Have a team meeting every single day. Just for 15 minutes – but make those minutes count.

Improvement and costs.

▶ Take a firm and consistent line on employee theft – always sack proven thieves and prosecute wherever possible.

▶ Walk the fine line between minimising customer theft and creating an unappealing high-security atmosphere.

▶ Prosecute shoplifters.

▶ Anything the customer doesn't see only ever needs to be functional and cost effective.

▶ Try to get stuff done right first time – especially the solving of customer complaints.

▶ Negotiate everything.

▶ Pool resources with other local retailers.

▶ Swap cost-saving ideas with your neighbours.

▶ Keep track of all supplier rebates and discounts.

▶ Get more than one quote!

▶ Use email for as many of your communications as possible so long as doing so does not make you look cheap to the customer.

▶ When prioritising areas to look into for savings, concentrate first on your largest cost categories – a small success in one of those can be worth much more than a big success in a tiny cost category.

▶ Check any special group rates negotiated by your trade association.

▶ Listen to what customers tell you they think is important – anything they don't rate highly is probably not worth spending much cash on.

▶ Cut out the middleman wherever you can.

▶ New design graduates are a much better and more cost-effective option for your advertising and direct marketing than an ad agency is.

▶ When placing print orders or booking a TV or radio advert, always demand the agency discount – this is a 10 to 20 per cent discount that printers, radio stations and telly channels give to agencies. Just because you book direct doesn't mean you shouldn't get the discount too.

▶ Make good use of government employment programmes but listen to your conscience – if it looks like slave labour it probably is slave labour.

▶ If an employee isn't pulling their weight and you have tried hard to help them then you have to let that person go.

▶ Do any members of the team have any skills that might mean you can avoid hiring in a tradesman? (Pay the employee a proper bonus for any above and beyond jobs that they do though.)

▶ Measure where your customers are coming in from – improve or cut any activity that is not driving traffic.

▶ If you pay employees a profit-related bonus then that will in itself help limit some of the unnecessary expenditure – so long as you are also sharing the store profit and loss information.

▶ Use your ideas programme to harvest all the cost-saving ideas the team can come up with.

▶ Consider sharing savings with the employee who identified them.

▶ Be nice to suppliers and let them pay for stuff if they want to.

▶ Get rid of the waste – any process that does nothing for customers, or for you, just has to go.

▶ Look at these processes all the time.

▶ Reuse things whenever you can.

▶ Teach employees how to promote the business when they are outside of work.

▶ Renegotiate all contract renewals; insurance premiums especially can be slashed at these times.

▶ Ask the team if they know a way to get hold of something cheaper – years ago when we bought a horribly expensive colour photocopier it wasn't until the behemoth was delivered that one of the warehouse lads said 'New copier? I could have got you a discount – my Dad is regional director for Canon'.

PART THREE – **CUSTOMER**

Make me happy and I will give you my money

8

How to make more money

Customer loyalty is a myth, a consultant's pipe-dream. A nonsense. Trying to gain it, trying to buy it, trying to bribe customers is ridiculous, costly and pointless. A customer is no more loyal to Top Shop than she is to New Look. She'll happily shop both of a Saturday afternoon. My Nan, getting on though she may be, is no more loyal to Waterstones Oxford than she is to Borders Oxford (separated, as they are, by just 50 yards) – she'll shop 'em both.

Some of us might be loyal to our brand of breakfast cereal or toothpaste but we are not loyal to the names above the door of the various places we can buy them from. But even that brand loyalty is moot in an age when choice is ubiquitous and consumption predicated on disposable living. Sure, personally I've never forgiven Colgate for discontinuing my favourite sub-brand of toothpaste and actively seek out remainder stock of the green nectar from discount stores (I have 20 packs in reserve right now – thank you Savers in Barnet) but if Macleans come up with a toothpaste that tastes and performs as well as the green one – it's so long Colgate and not a second's pang of regret will be felt.

This is the reality my friends. Time to find a new one and here it is.

First visit advantage

First visit advantage is a move on from the blunt definition of customer loyalty. Traditional customer loyalty holds that customers will always come to you to satisfy their needs in your product areas. To the exclusion of all other stores. Nonsense. The world doesn't spin like that.

But what if we can build formats so great and customer experiences so compelling that people are prepared to give us the first opportunity to sell to them on any given shopping trip? That they will come to you first before moving on to your competitor's stores. There is loads of evidence – including really strong stuff from Paco Underhill's Envirosell team – that shows a massive percentage of customers will buy, or return to buy, the first item they really like on a shopping trip. And common sense says getting the first crack at satisfying customers' needs is a good thing.

The idea of first visit advantage is that customers enjoy the experience in your store so much that whenever they plan a DIY project, or want to buy some clothes, or want to make something nice for tea, yours is the store they visit first. Having this advantage leads to a much greater probability that the customer will buy from you in preference to a competitor. It is a very powerful concept.

First visit advantage can be won in three ways: through promotion, through preference for your format and through the human experience in your store. Remember especially that the human parts of that equation are always the most powerful.

Case study 8.1 *Smart Retail*: Becoming first

One of Europe's leading DIY businesses discovered in 2006 that customers were only putting 20 per cent of their total project spend with that retailer. Customers were actively driving to these stores, parking the car, trundling round the aisles and still only spending a fifth of their budget for that project at that store.

Big chunks of their project spend was found to be going to specialists in tiles, flooring, kitchens, bathrooms and gardens. Customers only came to these huge DIY sheds for the niggly extras, cheap offers on base materials and for tools.

A legitimate interpretation of that situation would be that customers were almost begrudging having to give this retailer even that share of the project spend.

The response has been to make big investments in improving the in-store format of those specialist areas (bathrooms, flooring etc.) and in significantly raising standards of customer service. To an extent these changes are now paying off. However, I believe this particular retailer needs to do much, much more on service standards before it can undo its losses to the specialists (and that's why I've not named the retailer in this case study).

The four rules of performance improvement

There is no secret to performance improvement. The techniques can all be learned. But just as some racing drivers can make an identical piece of metal move consistently faster than that of a team mate, so it is that some retailers are able to improve performance better than anyone else. I've known a few racing drivers over the years and the best of them have one thing in common: consistency of line. They take the right line through more corners more times than anyone else. That's it, nothing magic or secret or unknowable. The same thing holds true when it comes to performance improvement. There is no secret; it's about getting the details right and paying attention to the fundamentals.

The rules of performance improvement are beautifully simple and there are only four of them.

To improve performance you can:

1   Sell to new customers.

2   Sell more in each transaction.

3   Persuade existing customers to return to your store more often.

4   Improve margin by cutting overheads and improving sales quality.

This is another of those 'it's not rocket science' moments. The challenge is of course in understanding how best to apply each rule. The chapters in this part of *Smart Retail* deal with those things you can do to produce direct results from applying these rules to your customers. People and store issues also have a part to play in the successful application of these rules of course, but it is what you can do directly for the customer that has the most significant impact.

Priorities

If I was forced to choose just one of the four rules of performance improvement over all others, the one I would pick is 'Sell more in each single transaction'. Driving up average transaction values

Driving up average transaction values is all about maximising every opportunity.

is all about maximising every opportunity. That in itself is a powerful business improvement philosophy. 'Make the very best of every customer who walks in' is your first consideration.

People make the difference to great customer experiences

'Of course, what rapidly becomes apparent in a service business like ours is that you can only look after the customer by looking after your staff. So, the route to creating value for the customers is through management of your people. Good retailers always understand this instinctively and we, at Tesco, regard it as a major priority.' Sir Terry Leahy – CEO, Tesco

Quote taken from the fantastic *Uncommon Practice* by Andy Milligan and Shaun Smith (Prentice Hall, 2002)

Here's a good illustration of the truth that people are a critical factor. Bookselling on the high street, seemingly against the odds, has survived the Amazon phenomenon despite books being generally cheaper to buy online. In fact, what has happened is the reverse: Amazon, aided too by the 'Harry Potter effect' has helped to stimulate overall demand for books, perhaps reminding a market blinded by technology that reading was a lost pleasure? Great book retailers, Waterstones, Barnes & Noble, Borders and a whole army of great independents, recognised that they needed to change – that they needed to offer a more significant added-value experience.

And as those retailers did so, customers began to remember how nice it was to be in a bookshop, to browse and to touch and feel. Even though they could buy the same books much more cheaply at Amazon or even

Asda they seemed to value the warm, human experience in a real book-shop. The sector is really very healthy – value and price are not the same thing, and the old truism that people like people seems to hold fast.

9

Great customer service

I got a bit of stick after the first edition for copping out a little here. I talked about how customer service isn't an add-on activity – I said it was *the* activity and that great service quality came from everything you do as a retailer. Some readers, understandably, felt that I was hiding the secret to great service quality ... well, thing is, there isn't one. What I can do though, is to point out more of the places in which you can work to create overall improvements.

First and foremost it's worth talking about why most service quality initiatives fail. Sometimes a marketing team will take a look at their list of 'things to do' and one of the bullet-points will read 'make customers love us again' and they'll commission an agency, or two, to come over and create some sort of 'service event'. They'll then have jolly good fun taking this event around the store estate and they'll say to people 'we order you, albeit in a nice way, to smile at customers and be their friends and love them so they will love us'.

And these one-off initiatives often deliver big early uplifts in customer satisfaction – then those gains die off, usually quickly, and before long everything returns to normal. That's because the focus always moves on: no matter how committed a retailer is to raising customer service quality, there is always another issue waiting in the wings to occupy the minds of management and teams.

Permanent improvements in standards of customer care have to be earned from the ground up – you can't change things by layering initiatives onto unstable foundations. Building from the ground up is harder work but ultimately more satisfying because gains become self-sustaining and permanent. Dieting is a good analogy – crash dieting creates instant weight loss but almost always results in a net weight gain once the focus slips. Changing eating behaviours, seeking support, changing attitudes to food and learning about nutrition means slower weight loss but, for the vast majority, permanent and self-sustaining success.

'Self-sustaining' is the key phrase – a successful assault on changing the behaviours and relationships that lead employees to *want* to deliver great customer care becomes a positive, viral thing: changes feel good, staff get more from their employment experience and customers get more from shopping the store. Even better – these changes reinforce each other in a virtuous circle:

Happier staff → better customer experience → happier customers → better interaction with staff → happier staff . . . and round and round it goes.

Better still, that loop delivers gains in revenue and profit and draws in improvements in employee retention and reductions in employment costs. It is an absolute win–win.

One team at a time

As a store manager you might now be thinking that there's nothing you can do to influence levels of service quality in your store, that it's all down to centrally-dictated policies. Well, you can and you can't influence service standards – your leadership is absolutely vital in creating a good place to work and in filling it with a motivated team. Doing that following the advice in the *Team* part of the book will make a massive impact on how it feels to come and shop your store – with all the benefits that generates. Where things get tricky is in navigating your way through the negative stuff that you're sometimes asked to implement. A great example of this was seen at electrical retailer Powerhouse before that business, funnily enough, got into serious financial trouble: at one point all staff were forced to ask every customer if Powerhouse could please sell them their gas and electric. It was really pushy, staff felt uncomfortable and customers absolutely loathed being asked. And then they went to Comet or Currys instead.

Faced with something like that, as a manager, what do you do? To be honest the right thing when it gets that extreme is to read the writing on the wall and jump ship. For most of you though, any negatives impacting on the employment experience, and therefore the customer experience, will stem from good, old-fashioned, well-meaning but poorly informed policies – unforeseen results of otherwise sensible decisions. Your role as a manager is to try to make these work, at the same time as feeding back your experiences and explaining why such-and-such isn't perhaps the world's greatest idea. Get customer and team comments, show you have tried to make a policy work and create a compelling case, with alternative solutions in it. Then talk to your bosses.

Case Study 9.1 *Not Smart Retail*: Not thinking

Here's a good example, and a typical one too, of well-meaning management tomfoolery ruining customer experiences. Somebody, somewhere at Lloyds TSB thinks the following is good customer service, that it's helping customers, who are missing out, to be brought into the family. Thanks to my mate Neil Degg for this perfect illustration.

> My bank (Lloyds TSB) phoned me up yesterday at work and said 'I can see from your records, Mr Degg, that you do not wish to be contacted.'
>
> Erm.
>
> The phone nearly went down there and then but I was intrigued as to where the call was leading so I said 'Yes' and obviously I got all the spiel about not passing on personal information to third parties and only contacting you about things that would be relevant to you, blah de blah de blah. This went on for what felt like ten minutes and I rapidly slipped into that thing of not really listening and just saying 'Yeah' and 'OK' even though I was probably just biroing a smiley face on the blob of Blu-Tack on my desk.
>
> Anyway, the next (and only) question I get is 'So do you want me to change the database and allow us to contact you?'

'NO!'

'OK, thanks for your time, Mr Degg. Goodbye!'

What's all that about then? Tuesday afternoon – hmmm, bored are we? Why do they bother mithering existing customers? Why not phone up some NatWest customers instead and see if you can poach them?

Sheeeeessh.

Neil's right too – I'd love to do a follow-up survey (erm, by telepathy I guess) and find out just how many customers felt anywhere from irritated to proper-angry after that intrusion. I suspect the total percentage would be high.

We need answers on this customer service thing

I know, I know, you're still thinking I'm on a cop-out here. Right: here's a bunch of stuff you can do to make sure that you and your team are deliv-

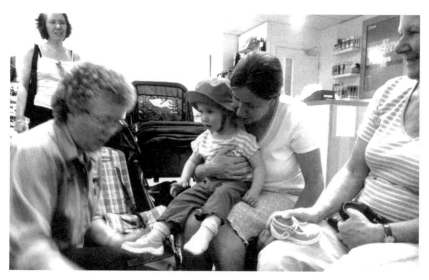

Picture: Koworld

Great customer service makes people feel good about your store

ering great customer experiences and that you send your customers away delighted.

Employee satisfaction

I've probably gone on a bit about this but it's worth saying again: put into practice the stuff in the *Team* part of this book. The most effective way to improve service quality is to improve the satisfaction of your team. Having a reward and bonus programme based around customer satisfaction scores can be really effective too. It helps your team to make a direct link between how they look after customers and what goes into their own pockets.

Simplify

Be simple and straightforward for customers – make promotions easy to understand and simple to redeem. Use plain language in your advertising and communications, be clear about what you can and can't do.

Deliver on the promise of your Big Idea

Whatever that big idea is, it is also a promise to your customers that you will be what you say you are! If a customer is coming to your store expecting you to be this big idea then make sure that you really are and keep looking out for all those things you could be doing that serve to support and emphasise that.

Meet the fundamental discovery need

All shopping is about discovery (see the *Store* part): help your customers to make those great discoveries. Surprise, delight and 'wow' them with recommendations and formats in which the brilliant and the great rise to the top. Make the store easy to move around, fill the place with great value and make sure people can see it. Be proud of your stock, make heroes out of the amazing and brilliant, and above all these things make sure your people are knowledgeable, that they have access themselves to your product and that they are open-minded enough to listen to customers' real needs and then to find great ways to meet those.

Be consistent

Make sure your team is in the lead every day – make sure you exceed company standards, stay on top of your game. And across the company ensure that the experience is great: every store, every time.

Fix problems directly

See, the thing is, we're all going to end up on *Watchdog* one day with Nicky Campbell greasily explaining to us that we are the devil incarnate. That's just the way the world is. But we can reduce our chances of that happening too often by accepting that we *will* make mistakes sometimes, and then by getting on and fixing those problems quickly, fairly and with a smile.

Feedback

Making it easy for customers to feed back to you is critical in improving service quality. If you haven't got a customer complaint process, one that's easy for customers to use, create one. Give customers quality surveys that they can fill in and send back to you. Give them pre-paid envelopes to make it even easier for them to do that. Give out your email address and your telephone number. Encourage complaints and think of them as free market research. Some customers will rant and rage but at the heart of almost every complaint is a truth that, once learned, will help you to make your business better. Oh, and it's far better that customers complain to you, and that you resolve their complaints, than it is for them to complain about you to their friends instead.

Encourage complaints and think of them as free market research.

Be honest and open

If you don't know the answer to something – say so and then find out. Be ready to admit your mistakes and involve your team and your customers in fixing things and in improving the store. Have an open mind in all situations.

Don't pay sales commission

Put your people on individual sales commissions and some of them will shark your customers. That's simple, straightforward human nature. The best service organisations pay people bonuses based on customer satisfaction combined with something reflecting overall store–profit performance. Or just be a great employer and give your frontline people salaries. Some of the happiest, most satisfied customers in the US are customers of The Container Store: *'Our salespeople do not work on commission; instead, they're either salaried or paid by the hour with wages far above the retail industry norm. Therefore, they often work together in teams to find that complete solution for the customer, which allows them to spend as much time as necessary to help customers find what they need.'* That's simple retail right there.

Smile and be nice, dammit!

Okay, I'm not talking the rictus-grins of the retail damned – but do try to put your troubles to one side when dealing with your team and your customers. Use the great opportunity you have as a retailer to talk to people, to enjoy their company and appreciate the fact that you're not stuck in an office staring at the same ten faces all day every day and fearing your turn on the tea-run. Retail is ace like that – for every mean-spirited or rude customer, you'll work with a hundred who are good fun, who are loving being out and spending money. Shopping *is* fun – have fun yourself you old misery.

Respect your people and they'll respect your customers

Treat people how you yourself would like to be treated. Be nice, be respectful, give the benefit of the doubt and remember that your people are grown-ups. Treat your team that way and they'll do the same with your customers.

Living and breathing it

Every decision you make must be in the context of 'will this be good for our customers?'. Every person you hire must be someone you think customers will enjoy being served by and every process, promotion and event you choose must be for the benefit and delight of customers. Great customer service is not a bolt-on activity, it is the *only* activity. As such every word in this book is written in the context of great customer service.

If service is poor business will suffer.

If service is poor business will suffer. Customers have less patience for poor service than ever before and Britons have even learned how to complain. If there *is* one secret to great customer service it is the knowledge that great customer service begins with your people.

Great moments

What is great customer service? It's hard to define but I tend to feel that it's mostly about empathy, common sense, turning the cheek and the banter on and off at the right time, delivering on your big idea and making sure people leave your store with a smile on their face. The best way to illustrate what customer service is, is with some real examples from our service quality survey.

Lush – Sheffield (UK)

Nathan Ditum's experience

I went in to buy a birthday present for my sister-in-law, loaded down with a pram (Maddy) and a hyperactive four-year-old (Jay). The girl in there was really friendly and polite – it didn't feel like she was being pushy, just helpful. She helped me choose a gift pack for the pressie (as a regular customer I know Lush's stock, but she knew all about which was best for sensitive skin, hairtype etc.) and to choose a bath bomb as an extra for Sarah. Jay's been in before and he loves taking the bath bomb samples and watching them fizz up – this ace girl not only got some water out to occupy him so he wasn't buzzing around the shop while I was looking around, but chucked a sample of his favourite one into the bag for free, and then even dug out a baby one for Maddy.

Me and Jay were chatting about how nice she was all the way home. It's the sort of customer service encounter that – small though it is in the big scheme of things – puts a big smile on your face and can make your day.

Specsavers – Cheltenham (UK)

Melanie Taylor's experience

[I] sat on my metal-framed specs a while ago. Annoyed that I'd have to wear my slightly 'pants' spare pair for a few days, I went with the broken ones in hand to Specsavers in Cheltenham, from whence they were purchased. It was a Sunday morning and the store was pretty busy.

'I've sat on my specs,' says I, 'Do you think they look fixable?'

The lass on the front desk examines the severely knackered-looking specs. I fully expect her to say, 'They might be too bent to straighten out again,' but instead she says, 'Yes, no problem at all.'

'How long will it take?' I ask, thinking I'll have to come back after work the next day, or even later in the week.

'Oh, we're a bit busy – could you come back in 20 minutes or so?'

'Oh! Sure!'

When I return to pick them up, the store is still very busy. The same lass immediately turns to pick up my specs as I approach the counter. 'Here you are!' she says brightly, passing my specs back. They have been so well repaired they look like a brand new pair. I am amazed. 'How much will that be?' I ask, digging in my pocket for a tenner. 'No charge!' she says brightly. 'We don't charge for minor repairs if you bought your specs from us. Would you like a slip case for your spare pair?' and hands me a soft case so that I can take my crappy old pair home without scratching them.

Now *that's* what I call good service! And that's why I have gone back to them to try contact lenses.

The Warehouse – Christchurch (NZ)

Sty Smith's experience

A few weeks ago I was trawling through the CDs and DVDs on special offer at this no-frills giant store. I came across a Riverdance DVD – knowing that my wife likes Riverdance I decided to buy it for her, especially as it was on at a bargain NZ$15. The DVD wasn't the original one released when Riverdance was first launched but was a more recent show filmed in Geneva with different dancers.

While I was paying I mentioned to the girl on the counter that I had really been looking for the original version but this was a good deal anyway. She then said that she was sure they had the original in somewhere for the same price. She checked the computer and confirmed that it was indeed in stock and then spent ten minutes with me searching through all the places it could have been out on the shelves and in the bargain displays, all to no avail.

She then very kindly offered to keep an eye open for it and give me a call if she came across it: she took a record of my phone number and that was that for a couple of weeks. I then, one day, got a very clear message with her name, the store, the fact that she had located the DVD and had put it aside for me for a week and I could come in and collect the film when it suited me.

That felt like proper service and I've felt good vibes about that store ever since.

Elif Restaurant – Liverpool (UK)

Nik Borton's experience

We went to the new Turkish restaurant near us. Nice food, fairly promptly served in a dining room presided over by the eccentric and enigmatic Turkish owner. Bellies full, we made to pay and we pointed out that they'd missed a round of drinks off the bill as we handed over our credit card. After the owner had corrected the bill he wrapped it around our card and said 'We don't take cards at the moment, so take the bill with you and pay next time.'

Too right there'll be a next time: with that one gesture – and refusing to hear of us walking the whole five minutes to an ATM – he's guaranteed that we'll be back at least once, and has gotten himself word of mouth advertising into the bargain.

Anthropologie – New York (US)

Chris Ahchay and Sarah Treacy's experience

We'd bought some jeans and that from Gap, wandered out of the shop and off on our merry little way without really thinking anything more about it. As you do. Unfortunately Gap had forgotten to take the security tags out of our clothes so in the next shop we went into we set off their alarms.

Now, maybe it's just indicative of what I've come to expect in a big town (a shrug of the shoulders and a cursory bag-search if you're lucky) but the security chap in the shop took one look at the Gap bag, said 'Oh, that'll be the security tags then, they're always doing that.' He then sent one of the shop girls off to find a pair of scissors and then spent five minutes carefully unfolding our Gap stuff, finding the tags and cutting them out before folding them all up again and sending us off on our way. All while having a perfectly pleasant conversation with us about our stay in New York and what not.

We bought some candles.

The shop was just one of those little boutique shops in Soho that, if it hadn't been for this chap at the door, we'd have wandered into, had a cursory look round and then buggered off again without buying anything.

Focus DIY – Berkshire (UK)

Rachel Maskelyne's experience, as told by husband Paul

My missus went in to buy a few bits and pieces with her old man as he has a pensioners' 10 per cent discount card that he'd gotten from his local branch. They got to the till and the apologetic girl there explained that the discount cards are only valid in Focus stores where there's a competing DIY store within a mile and how this is all a bit rubbish really but the till won't let her put it through.

She then asks if we had moved house recently as, if we had, she could give us a different 10% discount card that will work in any Focus for six months. Rachel explained that we had indeed moved recently, but the discount card we had from them had expired a few weeks previously (hence trying to use father-in-law's instead). 'Oh!' she says, 'I'll pretend I didn't hear that second bit' and signed us up for another six-month discount card.

Victoria's Secret – Pennsylvania (US)

Steve Trimble's experience

I'd not long been married and, young and naive, was looking for a Christmas gift for my new bride, wandering around the Exton Square Mall like a deer caught in headlights. Exhausting the cooking, candle and housewares stores, I come up on a Victoria's Secret ... ah ha! So I wander in and naturally feel a bit awkward but I push through the store looking (not touching!). I get this idea that I should get my wife some of those thigh-high stockings but unfortunately I can't find them, so I approach the counter.

'Hi, yes, I'm looking for stockings for my wife.'

Sales girl asks: 'What kind? We have many different types of stockings.'

Me: 'Ummm ... like the ... kind ... ummm'

Her: 'Oh you mean like these?' as she promptly lifted her skirt a little to reveal a spectacular pair of legs, clad in a breathtaking pair of stockings.

I can't quite recall what happened next but before I knew what was what, my credit card was out on the counter and then I was walking out of the store not only with the stockings but with a bag stuffed full of lotions, creams and other crap I had no idea I was buying.

Author's note: I know this one might be a bit on the 'not PC' side and all that, but it's still a good example.

Shoe Clinic – Westfield Mall, Riccarton (NZ)

John and Niamh Guy's experience

Niamh is nearly four and as such regularly needs new shoes. With summer coming to an end we wanted to buy her some new 'proper' shoes. Previously we have bought ClarksJ but this time we wanted to try the Startright brand instead as we had heard very good things about it – it's a UK brand I believe and Shoe Clinic were the only stockist in town.

When we got in there, unfortunately they had stopped carrying them in this branch. Our disappointment turned to happiness when the assistant kindly offered to get a couple of pairs in stock for us to try out. The next few minutes were spent having Niamh's feet measured and then looking at the catalogue and choosing a couple of styles and colours we liked, and we left them with our phone number.

A few days later the call was received that the order had arrived: we had a couple of types to try.

Next weekend we went in and tried the shoes on Niamh. The whole experience was great, they're really a sports shoe shop and sell lots of proper sports shoes, so Niamh was able to walk on the treadmill they usually film people's feet on. This was a great distraction for a three-year-old and allowed us to evaluate the fit etc.

We joined their free loyalty scheme: spend NZ$500 and get a NZ$50 voucher.

A few weeks later Niamh suddenly needs football boots for soccer at school – I get the call on a Tuesday afternoon and am told she needs the boots before Wednesday afternoon. To make things worse she is at kindergarten on the Wednesday until soccer starts, meaning she can't actually go into town to buy boots.

On my own, I go looking in the mall for boots – not easy as she is an infant UK size nine, which is small (think of those little boots you see mad people have hanging from their rear view mirrors). I try the obvious mega-sized sports shop: no joy.

I then try the Shoe Clinic we went to before but they have the same slight problem: nothing that small in stock, best they have are two pairs of adidas that appear to be a size too big.

The same assistant from the earlier visit is very helpful: she remembered our previous visit and was able to remind me of the exact sizes we had ordered. We dig out the brochures and check all the available models from all the suppliers, Nike, adidas, Puma, and determine that there are only a couple of options that may be small enough. Phone calls are made to other local branches – no joy with stock, phone calls are also made to the central office to check availability and unfortunately no luck there either.

Here's where the service kicks up a gear ...

I was offered the option of taking a pair of the possibly too-large adidas boots 'on approval'. I went so far as to reassure her that we'd only be trying them on carpet etc. but this didn't seem to concern them. I offered to pay first, but instead they took my credit card details and said if I liked the shoes just call them and they'd put the payment through.

The boots were great – size-wise nothing a thick pair of socks didn't cure. I popped in the next day, paid for the boots under strict orders from the Mrs to get the loyalty points, which I of course forgot all about. After paying, the assistant proactively reminded me that I was a loyalty card holder and got me to give her the details so the transaction could be credited to us.

Brilliant, brilliant, brilliant service: and Niamh loves her soccer boots.

Picture: Elaine Guy

Happy Niamh

CHAPTER TEN

A little bit about strategy and why it's worth bothering reading about

The simplicity of retail sometimes chokes strategists, CEOs and commentators – 'Surely a business turning over hundreds of millions of pounds has to be doing something really clever and really complicated?'

Nope. They're just selling stuff to people who want it. They're doing it consistently well and within a great format. Your big idea is, of course, utterly integral to the strategy chosen. That said, there are broadly three generic strategic directions available to us retailers:

1   **Cost-led**

This is where the action has been over the last twenty years, and evidence suggests that it's likely to remain so. Essentially, a cost-focused strategy is one in which all areas of cost are streamlined, efficiencies are hunted down and savings used to drive down prices to customers. EDLP (everyday low pricing) is one expression of this strategy.

Retailers operating this strategy include: Wal-Mart, Aldi, Primark, New Look

2   **Differentiated**

This is about added-value – finding a way to be different from the competition in a way that customers will appreciate and pay for. So you might not be the lowest cost option but you will be targeted by customers because something else in your mix appeals to them. Added value might include convenience, advice and ambience (especially in fashion). Or you might just have identified something utterly unique.

Retailers operating this strategy: Spar (convenience), Carphone Warehouse (advice), Fortnum & Mason (exclusivity)

3   Segmented

A segment-focused strategy is one in which the retailer concentrates all their efforts on fulfilling the needs of a very specific market segment. 'Niche' is sort of the same strategy except applying to product rather than customer. This strategy often requires elements of the first two to work – so, for example, you might be the lowest cost retailer looking after the needs of people called Colin. I dunno, selling them name plates with 'Colin' written on and personalised stationary and that. Or you might be a specialist retailer offering Colins goods with 'Colin' written on that they had never known existed, or perhaps be the first retailer to Colins with late opening hours and local branches.

Often a segmented strategy comes about as a result of an existing retailer looking for new opportunities: Tesco Metro, for example, is a Tesco format that exists purely to satisfy high street shoppers in towns.

Retailers operating this strategy: Thornton's (chocolate lovers), Long Tall Sally (tall women), Tie Rack (people in a hurry to buy a dreadful comedy tie)

Summary

What it boils down to is that a strategy is really all about working out where the opportunity might be, finding out if customers are likely to, literally, buy into the strategy and then creating a format that exploits that opportunity. It is honestly about Fisher Price-sized decision-making: all primary colours and really obvious once you've had a play with it. The challenge, as I've stressed throughout, is to hang a big idea onto your strategy and then convert that into a consistent and compelling format that everyone – you, your colleagues, your customers and your stakeholders – can buy into.

Other stuff that's worth knowing

Format

Technically, your format is simply the environment you sell your product in. We've all got that one pal who is able to take a simple gift and wrap it so wonderfully that the whole receiving and unwrapping process becomes a really great experience – she's used the same basic ingredients everyone else does but put them together in such a way as to leave an end result that is so much more than the sum of those parts. Great retail formats are much like that – the parts are available to everyone, it's how you put them together that makes the difference and gives you the edge. The biggest variable in that list is the people you put in that box: your team is capable of making the biggest single difference to your format's success.

Location

Format and location are very closely tied together – a small store, for example, built for high volume and dependent on passing impulse-trade must deliver a format that can be made to work in expensive primary high-footfall locations.

Specialists and generalists

You can then further break down these strategies into a specialist or generalist proposition. Generalists include the grocers, the variety stores and so on. Specialists, well, they specialise in one area. Let's take videogames: generalists such as Tesco and Woolworths *can* sell you a videogame, whereas the specialists Game and Gamestop will *only* sell you videogames.

Independents

Let's say you're an independent fashion retailer – you're a generalist in that you sell all sorts of clothes, from various brands, but you can still choose to specialise in one area. Choosing to create a specialist part of your reputation can be really powerful – in this example you might decide to offer the best range of party dresses in town every autumn, ready for the

Christmas party season. You might choose to specialise in offering a really exciting range of shoes from independent designers. Whatever you choose you then have a great story to tell customers.

Case study 10.1 Smart Retail: Specialism at Tony Hillam's

For twenty years Tony Hillam ran a hardware store located just outside Cleckheaton in Yorkshire. Tony retired a few years back but still, purely for the fun of it, works holiday relief in the store he sold. That is retail passion in a nutshell and should tell you a lot about the type of retailer Tony is.

The Cleckheaton store, which still bears the name Tony Hillam, has two complementary specialist reputations. In the winter, Tony Hillam's is the best place to buy your Calor gas, but it is the summer specialism that works so well for the store. In summer customers travel miles, sometimes fifty or more, to talk lawnmowers with the Hillam team. Tony stocks an extensive range of models, parts and accessories. On most lines Hillam's matches the equivalent B&Q price and on some he beats them. Crucially though the store's reputation allows it to stock additional high-margin specialist models that would be slow movers in one of the big DIY sheds.

It is not just the choice and range that attracts customers, it is also the ready supply of friendly and trustworthy advice that is always on offer in the store. Truth is we English love a mower and can't help wanting a lawn beast that is better than our neighbours' machine. Tony Hillam's specialism helps create a pleasant place in which customers can indulge that little garden pleasure – an environment that makes the buying, running and maintaining of these machines a treat.

Added value

Literally this is about putting something extra on the table that customers might value. Below is a list of added value you could put into practice in your stores (also check the 27 promotion types listed later for more ideas).

Here in black and white, this list feels very ordinary – it *is* pretty ordinary as it goes. The magic comes from the way in which you and your teams put this stuff into practice. A 'tip sheet' sounds a bit dull – but written with passion, fun, energy and a bit of wit it can be a really welcome part of the customer experience. Do these things consistently, have them support your big idea and they carry significant power.

> **The magic comes from the way in which you and your teams put this stuff into practice.**

Here's that list:

- ▶ Recommendations
- ▶ Product demonstrations
- ▶ Masterclass technique demonstrations
- ▶ Product training for customers
- ▶ Tip sheets
- ▶ After-sales service
- ▶ Trade-in
- ▶ Expert staff
- ▶ Credit facilities
- ▶ Loan product availability
- ▶ Pre-order facilities
- ▶ Bespoke services such as tailoring
- ▶ Specialist product ordering
- ▶ Delivery services
- ▶ Free samples
- ▶ Try-before-you-buy
- ▶ Convenience
- ▶ Design services.

Case study 10.2 *Smart Retail*: Value equations

Staff cost money and sometimes it's easy for retailers to see the wages line on a Profit and Loss account only in terms of the hard figures. At a store committed to everyday low prices at all costs, the amount of revenue budgeted to cover staff costs might be as low as 4 or 5 per cent. One such retailer is Home Depot whose big idea is so entrenched in the idea of everyday low prices that it might not be able to afford to trade at all if it had a wage percentage much beyond that. Now that's fine when you're incredibly far ahead in an exponentially growing market (as Home Depot was in '90s US DIY) – frankly you could smear dog turds on the faces of your customers and they would still come to you for low prices and wide ranges. What Home Depot is experiencing now is the effect of a flattening market – all of a sudden customers start to subconsciously add things like service, advice, inspiration and shopping environment to their personal value equations and that's why Lowes, who appear to invest more in training and service, are picking up customers so rapidly.

What I need – what I want

When a person sets out on a shopping trip, they do so with a set of needs begging to be satisfied. Part of our job as retailers is to try to second-guess the most likely of these needs and build our stores, our big idea, our formats and our strategies around meeting them.

It's a tough exercise, this one – I always ask my clients to brainstorm and write down as many of the needs they believe their customers might possibly have. Instinctively most retailers kind of know what these are – but articulating them is a struggle.

So why bother? At its most basic, understanding your customers' likely needs makes it easier for you to sell them stuff by addressing those needs.

Here are some exercises I use with clients. The first seems a bit silly at first but give it a go before reading the 'reveal'. Try to do this in a group if possible – better ideas tend to emerge that way.

Needs Exercise Part 1 **Glass**

Fetch a drinking glass and put it on the table in front of you. Set a timer for five minutes and then write down all the things you think that glass could possibly be used for. Pick it up, handle it, think about what you could do if you broke it.

Done live, and in groups, the longest list of different uses I've had is 54.

Reveal

Okay, time's up: take a look at your list, look at the progression of uses on it – you'll have uses like 'drink out of it' and 'pen holder' up near the top and then, closer to the bottom, the mad stuff will appear such as 'anti-burglar device (smashed in a doorway)' and 'wasp prison'.

Okay, more analysis on that in a moment but first you need to do Part 2.

Needs Exercise Part 2 **Shirt**

Do the same thing as with the glass but this time use a shirt instead.

Reveal

Again you'll have a nice mixture of obvious 'to wear it' and lateral 'to create an instant disguise'. Now, what I'd like you to do is to look at both lists and next to each use write down a need that use could satisfy. So with the glass and 'drink out of it' the need might be 'to quench thirst'. Then do the same again but this time add a second 'need' to each line. So you might then have 'drink out of it' and 'quench thirst' plus 'to wash down some headache pills'.

Those second ones are much harder to do but still represent a legitimate need. Take a look at the lists – the 'uses' there can be thought of as your customers' actions such as 'bought a TV' or 'enquired about contact lenses' and the needs are, well, needs. So, starting from customer actions you see every day, you might have 'bought a TV' and 'because I thought a HD screen would make my DVDs look better' plus 'because the World Cup is coming soon'.

Needs Exercise Part 3 **My store**

Now, with unlimited time, write down all the possible things customers could use your store for, including listing all the different broad categories of products you sell and services you provide.

Then take five of those 'uses' and list at least ten 'needs' that your customers could possibly be satisfying by using your store for that purpose.

Needs Exercise Final Part | Action

By now you should be buzzing with real customer needs – let's have a crack at using that to learn something useful about your store.

Choose a section of your store or a particular range of items.

Consider

▶ What are the needs of customers shopping this section?

▶ How are you satisfying those needs?

▶ How does this fit with the big idea?

▶ What needs are going unsatisfied?

▶ How clear is our added value or specialism in this area? (if these apply)

▶ What can we change to meet a wider range of needs, to better meet existing needs and to improve the performance of that part of the store?

Cost-led positioning

Going back to the three strategic options I mentioned at the start of this chapter, cost-led is the hottest retail strategy of the moment so it's worth spending a bit more time on it. Over the last decade, of all retailer types, it's the ones with a value positioning that have seen the most success.

Price competition

Price competition carries significant risks. When the big chains engage in a price war, competitive advantage is gained for a short time only. Price matching can be a dangerous activity – whenever you match a competitor's price it sends out a distinct message about your other prices.

Everyday low prices (ELP)

Everyday low pricing is an interesting modern pricing technique. It's also the best example of the failure of slavish dedication to a rigid price proposition. The theory of ELP is that every price in-store is as low as possible every day. Furthermore, prices will not be slashed during sale periods, indeed that there will be no more sales at all – just the lowest prices every day.

US-based Wal-Mart are often credited as the pioneer of ELP. Founder Sam Walton would almost certainly have suggested that all Wal-Mart did was to take discounting and direct-from-manufacturer purchasing further than his competitors.

In the early 1990s Kingfisher companies – at the time B&Q, Woolworths, Superdrug and Comet – were among the first adopters of ELP in the UK. Others have since followed. Some retailers have always believed consistently low prices to be an honest customer proposition but have never felt the need to claim subscription to an evangelist philosophy.

The strongest myth surrounding the British interpretation of ELP is that offering everyday low pricing precludes the use of traditional price promotions. This interpretation of the technique is wrong. Not just wrong – it is anti-competitive advantage, because it ties one hand behind the retailer's back. I worked for Comet when the company first introduced ELP. A Kingfisher finance team attempted to codify ELP into a philosophy and then to interpret it as a mission applicable to the whole business. Pricing became the absolute focus of what we, as a retailer, did. Actually the mission at Comet was, or should have been: 'To sell a great range of electrical goods to delighted customers.' Pricing is an element of that mission, but so are fantastic, surprising and exciting promotions. To make pricing the absolute mission was wrong. It did not provide competitive advantage.

I am always mistrustful of attempts to shoehorn simple common sense into complex strategy. At Comet we interpreted ELP as meaning all prices would be monitored against those of major competitors, then adjusted our prices to match or beat these price points. In addition, each key product category would feature at least one product priced lower than any entry price-point offered by our competitors. The product would then remain at that category-killing low price every day. So, for example, we offered a 14″ portable colour TV at £99 when the previous entry price-point for this product was £109. All our competitors were at the £109 price when Comet introduced the category-killing £99 TV set. For how long do you suppose that competitive advantage lasted? A year? A season? Well Dixons, Currys and Argos cut their price point to match ours within weeks. All that happened was the whole sector now made £10 less profit for every one of those 14″ televisions sold. Don't forget, that's £10 lost out of gross margin.

Because we at Comet were committed to our misinterpretation of ELP it made it very hard to respond in turn to our competitors' actions. If we dropped our own price further it would have damaged the credibility of our ELP proposition, suggesting that our previous price was not the lowest everyday price after all. If we remained at £99, just like everyone else, we had no competitive advantage since pricing was our only competitive lever. Building the mission around ELP provided no competitive advantage at all. Yet ELP is still the focus at Comet today.

When rivals' store environments, prices and product ranges are so similar, there is a terrible fear that a customer will simply walk from store to store and buy on price alone. Comet, as do many others, believe that convincing the customer that their prices are always reliably low will ensure the customer comes only to them. I'm not sure that's very realistic given the amounts being spent on a single electrical product. Would you only check one store when spending £600 on a telly? ELP, as practised by many, is fatally flawed.

Would you only check one store when spending £600 on a telly?

Merchant dealing

I put the challenge of the £99/£109 14″ TV to a number of Britain's best retailers. They decided quickly that it would have been much more effective to have taken that TV and to have slashed a genuine deep cut off the price, say to £89, and then to have run that as a limited stock promotion. We would have negotiated a larger order with our original equipment manufacturer (OEM) and taken a bigger discount. That stock would make up the limited promotion. The promotion would then have been presented honestly to customers: 'Here's a fantastic deal we've negotiated specially for you: once it's gone, it's gone.' Indeed, this is exactly how Asda and Tesco have been beating the electrical retailers at their own game.

Yes the competition would still match our price, but by then we would have enjoyed at least two weekends of price leadership in this category. Also competitors would be forced to cut their margins from existing stock bought at their usual cost price so their profit per unit would actually be less than ours.

This bargain £89 TV would feature heavily in local press and radio advertising. Customers flicking through the local paper would see a bold, bright, honest advert. Many customers would bring forward an intended purchase as a result – 'Let's get one now and put it away for Tommy's Christmas pressy' and 'You've been on about a telly for the kitchen: shall we get one while this cheap deal is on?' And a significant number of customers would switch to Comet for this purchase because:

1   We made it easy for them.
2   We gave them a good reason to act now instead of tomorrow.

I strongly believe that real competitive advantage comes from maintaining honest everyday prices mixed with bargains. Quite simply, not ripping off the customer and retaining the ability to offer great, customer-delighting promotions. It is this approach, call it a philosophy if you want, that will enable your store to convince customers that you are honest people to do business with and that you are capable of exceeding their expectations on price.

Case study 10.3 Not Smart Retail: Training customers

All that advertising money we throw at customers is designed to get them to do the things we want them to. Well obviously. Throughout the '90s the biggest electrical retailers put trainloads of that cash into a single message: BUY ON PRICE, BUY ON PRICE, BUY ON PRICE. It was as if they'd had a collective madness and decided that the only thing customers should consider was the *price* of a cooker, a telly or whatever.

And we customers, because advertising works on us, did what the electrical retailers told us to do: we began to make our electrical consumer goods purchasing decisions based entirely on who could sell it to us for the least money.

And then the internet turned up. And us customers, so well trained by Comet, Dixons, Currys, Powerhouse and so on – well, we're not stupid. Just as we responded positively when told to only buy our electrical goods on price, so we responded positively to the collective message that the internet was the place to get the lowest prices.

And we stopped going to Comet, Dixons, Currys and Powerhouse, often buying instead from retailers on the internet.

And that's madness. The internet is a horrible place to buy big expensive stuff: you can't see it properly, you can't be sure the colour is as it appears on-screen, you can't even judge its size and bulk properly. But electrical retailers told you price, price, price was all that mattered. And they're still doing that.

The likes of Comet, especially, have a great opportunity to transform the customer experience when shopping for electricals but there seems to be real reluctance to take the risk. All the while, retailers such as Best Buy, Carphone Warehouse, John Lewis and Target are moving into the territory and getting really good at providing high levels of customer service in the form of quality advice, honest needs-analysis and superb after-sales support. Then at the truly price-sensitive entry level price-points Tesco, Wal-Mart, ASDA and Aldi are kicking traditional electrical retailers' bums.

My team reckon Comet would be our dream project – there is a massive potential there to learn from the Best Buys and the CPWs and to do something very special in the marketplace. We've asked if they'd let us but I'm not sure the team agree that the problem exists – despite Dixons' retreat from the high street and despite their own challenges to revenue and margin.

Value, bargains and honest pricing – the real ELP

Wander round the Wal-Mart near Hicksville (honest, it's on Long Island and I couldn't resist driving through a US town with a name like that) and you will see the pioneers of ELP doing ELP properly. It is not the rigid UK ELP approach but something much more instinctive. Yes, almost every product line is on the shelf at a reliably low price. But what shines out from these everyday low priced products are the mountainous piles of Wal-Mart special promotions at exceptionally low prices. Such promotions drive customer traffic very effectively. Actually, the customers' belief that Wal-Mart will always present them with exciting bargains is enough to drive traffic.

Making bargains the star

Even in a chain-store branch where you don't get to dictate prices you can still make bargains the star. There are always awesome offers in the price lists – these might be end-of-line items or even regular stock. Try pulling lots of the end-of-line product into your store from other stores around the company and then putting them out there in front of customers. Don't forget clearance and manager's specials too as bargains.

Make up some simple flyers featuring these star bargains. Hand these out on the car park and around town. If you have budget get them delivered with the local free papers too. Have your team point out the specials to every customer who comes through the door: 'Just in case you're in the market for X later, I wanted to tell you we have got them at Y price for a week or until the stock runs out.' That's not pushy – it's friendly, no-pressure selling.

Enthuse the whole team at your daily team meetings. Tell them about the day's top three bargains. Consider running a little incentive on those lines: a bottle of champagne goes to the person who sells the most over the weekend. A bottle of bubbly is just enough to help the team to take notice; it's a welcome treat for most, but it's not so much that sales people will mis-sell just to get it. Put flyers on doors and on the counter-top. Set up an A-frame outside if you can. Sometimes the council take offence to the presence of these A-frames but you won't know until they send you a nice letter and ask you to take it down, so go ahead and see what happens!

Pulling together the bargains is hard work. You must be inventive, on top of your inventory and ready to act fast. The work is worth it: you will drive customers into your store and the combination of honest pricing and real bargains will boost your reputation and your sales.

Bargains give you competitive advantage.

Bargains give you competitive advantage.

After reading this part of the first edition, lovely person Lyn Denny wrote to me and said *'I'm the owner of a small independent bookshop in Ireland. We've been open a year and things are going great. I bought your book in September and haven't looked back. We immediately introduced a bargains table and it has been the fastest selling area of my store ever since. We are delighted with it and so are our customers.'* Apart from me showing off a bit, why this is worth talking about is that Lyn's store isn't some down-market discount shop: Bookstór is a quality independent in a country that values literature highly (www.bookstor.ie).

Case study 10.4 *Smart Retail*: The democracy of bargains

In 2007 Primark, a proper no-nonsense bargain high-street fashion retailer, opened a 70,000 square foot flagship store on London's Oxford Street. Hilary Alexander, writing in the *Telegraph*, described the scenes on its first day: *'I have never seen anything like it. Even the first day of Harrods' sale is a vicarage tea party compared to the Primark pandemonium. By 11.15 am, there were still crowds three and four deep winding around the block on both sides and spilling onto the roadway as a mounted policewoman appealed for people to "please stay on the pavement". Security guards estimated tens of thousands had arrived by midday.'*

That mention of high-class department store Harrods is interesting – I've visited the Primark store a number of times since it opened and the customers in there are broadly the same people also shopping Selfridges, Debenhams, John Lewis, Next and Gap on the same street. The only customer group missing in Primark from those stores are the over-40s. Thing is, a Harrods customer is as keen on a bargain as anyone else. The millionaire enjoys being able to boast that he got a free diamond set into the face of his new Rolex Oyster, just as much as us lot do when we manage to blag a second mini-bag of peanuts on a flight. That's what

Wal-Mart, Primark and even Bookstór are tapping into: the buzz customers get from beating the system, from getting a real bargain. All customers love bargains: we are living in a bargain-driven culture.

Oi! That's my planet too!

I'm one of those people who grew up in the '70s and '80s in a world that believed consumption, at any rate, could be sustained for ever – too young to be bothered by the early 1970s oil shocks and too old to really 'get it' when late in the '90s environmental concerns began to gain credibility. Ten years on and even people like me have been forced to confront the reality that the blue and green ball upon which we stand isn't going to last if we keep kicking the crap out of it. Parallel to that we've begun to better understand the health benefits of eating better and walking about a bit more.

As retailers we are in the vanguard of consumption and we have got some serious thinking to do. Here and now I need to say that I am an unashamed capitalist and I believe strongly that the creation of wealth is a force for common good in the world. I'm also very supportive of the idea of globalisation: one planet, one nation – and why not?

So how does that square with the need for sustainability? Being one of the world's biggest sources of employment is a pretty good start – everyone is entitled to opportunity, dignity and the chance to earn a decent wage. Retail provides that and here's where we start to get to important stuff: time and time again it has been proved that retailers who treat their staff with respect and provide support and opportunities for self-fulfilment are the ones that customers prefer to shop with. On the customer side, growing awareness of the need for sustainable living is leading to a quiet revolution with our customers taking more and more of their spend to those retailers whose practices have the least negative impact on the planet.

We're really good, as an industry, at moving minds and influencing consumer behaviour – I believe the most forward-thinking retailers have an opportunity here to move customers even faster toward truly sustainable consumption. Why wait for consumer trends and government regulation to push us? Let's drive that change ourselves – not just because doing so, on a human level, is a feelgood thing but also because we can drive our businesses' success by doing so.

Broadly there are two routes open to retailers moving towards a sustainable position:

1 Commit the entire format to a sustainable position (Whole Foods Market, Lush, Abel & Cole).

2 Operate a traditional business but introduce a significant commitment to sustainable practices (Marks and Spencer, Waitrose, American Apparel).

Making these moves is a good community choice and a great human one too. Of course the usual caveats apply: choose your position carefully, communicate it well and above all be authentic – if you say you have a commitment to X then you must genuinely believe that commitment to be right or you run the risk of being 'found out'.

Case study 10.5 *Smart Retail*: Live it, breathe it, sell it

A key event in the early days of Whole Foods Market set the tone for the way in which this innovative food retailer sees itself as an integral part of the communities it serves. In 1981 a flood devastated Austin, Texas. Among the businesses ruined was WFM's then one and only store. The damage ran to $400,000 and without insurance the company looked doomed. Incredibly, customers and neighbours volunteered to join staff in clearing up the mess and in repairing the store – creditors and suppliers too provided breathing space for the business to get back on its feet, and less than a month after the disaster the store was up and trading again. Clearly, many people not employed by the company or financially dependent on it nevertheless felt they had a stake in the success of the business. If your local Tesco, ASDA or Sainsbury's suffered a flood, would you be there bailing out and mopping up?

Right from the start Whole Foods Market have had a clear vision that the food they sell should be grown responsibly, that local supply and the variety it produces, was preferable to the established mass-production model, and that employees and the community should be closely involved in the decision-making driving the business. They have a snappy line to sum up the way the business feels about its offer: Whole Foods – Whole People – Whole Planet.

What makes Whole Foods Market special is that they have made direct positive connections between 'doing the right thing' and making money. Just one small example of that: they offer financial support to employees whose choose to do voluntary community service – and they know that doing so makes both the employee and the community feel good. They also know that a happy, motivated employee helps the business to make more money and that an involvement with the community increases customer awareness. There is no cynicism in this: the top team want to be proud of the way in which they do business, they want to go to bed at night knowing that their working day has resulted in gain for everyone and in the right way.

I'm sure too that Whole Foods Market would be happy to carry on at their own rate, expanding when sensible to do so, and to a large extent minding their own business. However, the world has come into line with the principles driving Whole Foods Market and that should spark an interesting period for the business. The first WFM-branded store opened in the UK this year – a massive 80,000 square foot affair set in the iconic Barkers building in west London. I believe their sustainable and healthy approach will stir things up here just as they have in North America.

CHAPTER ELEVEN

Promote or die

Happy people

Carefully considered promotions can do masses for the business, and in conjunction with honest pricing and added value are essential performance improvement tools. There are of course those other factors to consider. Promotions without great customer service or attention to employee needs are near worthless. Poor, aggressive or sneaky promotions may bolster sales short term, but unhappy customers will rarely come back (breaking Performance Improvement Rule 3 – Persuade existing customers to return to your store more often), and will tell friends how rubbish you are (breaking Rule 1 – Sell to new customers). Unhappy employees will leave (that has a cost to you so breaks Rule 4 – Improve margin by cutting overheads and improving sales quality) or will not make any active selling efforts (breaking Rule 2 – Sell more in each transaction).

27 promotions

Here I have listed most of the popular promotion options open to retailers. I've included a table that makes it easy to see which promotions are good for achieving better performance under each of the four improvement rules. Finally the promotions planner will help you to see which promotions are right for you and when to run them.

Picture: Koworld

So long as they walk out with a bag!

1 Joint activity

Look for promotions you can share with either manufacturers or other retailers in your street. The obvious benefit is that you can pool costs and then afford to promote the activity more aggressively. An example of retailers engaging in joint activity might be a 'fun day' held within your shopping centre. A manufacturer and retailer joint activity could include manufacturer-supplied demonstrators, linked to a customer promotion and a manufacturer-funded staff incentive.

2 Displays in empty stores

I'd like to credit Rick Segel, 'one of the highest rated retail speakers in the world', with this brilliant idea. Find the landlords of an empty local retail unit and offer to put a display in the window. It makes the unit look more appealing for the landlord to rent and provides you with an excellent advertising space.

3 Sponsorship and community events

Don't always dismiss requests for sponsorship right out of hand. Sometimes a sensible sponsorship can do more for you than, say, your Yellow Pages advert. Businesses located at the centre of smaller communities gain most benefit from this form of promotion. Sponsoring events such as the town fun run or village fête makes a very strong statement about your commitment to the community. Many retailers have reported that the goodwill this creates does translate into sales.

4 Adverts in changing rooms

Cheap, easy and brilliant: put adverts in your changing rooms. Your customer is absolutely captive when they are in there and they have plenty of time to read. Think about featuring deals on accessories especially – customers who bite will be helping to push up your average transaction values.

5 Children's competitions

Maybe we are just a nation of soppy souls but children's competitions always work well. These can be very simple colouring or letter writing competitions. They could be themed: 'Draw or write a letter about your Mum for Mother's Day.' Local papers love this sort of thing. You have a good chance of getting a photo printed in the paper of the winner in your store.

6 Tip sheets

No matter what your product, you can easily produce useful tip sheets. A sheet of tips might seem a little uninspiring perhaps but time and again retailers tell me that customers go nuts for these, often citing them as the reason why customers come back. You can write tip sheets yourself or have a well-known expert do them for you at a cost. Formats can be anything from a full-colour booklet to a small card fixed to a shelf edge. My favourite format is loose A5 so that customers can take the tip sheets away with them. Here are some kinds of tip sheets:

▶ Recipes in a grocery.

▶ Recommendations and explanations in a wine merchant's shop.

▶ Hi-fi reviews in an electrical retailer.

▶ Home projects in a DIY store.

▶ Album reviews in a music shop.

7 Loyalty programmes

I don't believe that customers are ever loyal to the over-hyped special offers, magazines or bits of tinsel that most loyalty programmes consist of. In my wallet is a Nectar Card, a Tesco Club Card and a WHSmith Club Card. However, I'll happily spend money in Asda, buy a paper from my pal Ali round the corner or get a book in Waterstones. I'm not loyal even though I am in the loyalty programme. Neither am I alone in that response: few of these loyalty programmes really work. Customers are loyal to great friendly service, honest prices and nice places to shop – not to a plastic card.

The kind of loyalty programmes that do work are usually much simpler. Maybe a coffee house gives you a little card that they stamp each time you visit, and that entitles you to your sixth coffee free. Or a pizza company offers a loyalty bonus that allows you to get any pizza you want for free if you have saved up four receipts from previous orders. Those kind of loyalty programmes are unobtrusive, relatively low cost and customers really like them.

8 Customer-get-customer

You could offer existing customers a gift, store vouchers perhaps, if they recommend your store to a friend who then makes a purchase. All you need is a printed coupon which you give to every customer with their till receipt. The customer can fill in this coupon and give it to their friend. The friend brings in the coupon and it has the original customer's details still written on it so you can send them their reward.

If you are confident that people like you enough to recommend your store to friends, this is an effective way to make it easy for them to do exactly that.

9 Buy one get one free (or two-for-one, three-for-two etc)

In 2003 this was the UK's most popular promotional mechanism. If you can afford to run them, run them. Promote such offers heavily. Talk to your suppliers about funding either the offer, the advertising or both! If you can run a steady stream of good offers over a long period then this becomes even more effective because customers begin to pop in just to see what you've got on 'special'.

10 Sampler clubs

In some ways this is an extension of the tip sheet idea but with a chance for customers to actually try the product out. You take a group of your customers and sign them up to a hands-on sampling club. In that hi-fi store example you could hold regular demonstration evenings just for members, hold set-up lessons with an expert, make pre-ordering on limited edition products available to the members first and run exclusive offers.

11 Percentage off

Exactly what it says: you run either a day where everything is, say 10 per cent off, or you reduce a selection of lines for a limited period of time. It has become very hard to make such events really work though. The DIY sheds especially have trained customers to think that anything less than a 25 per cent discount isn't worth their while. Percentage-off promotions also make a negative statement about your usual prices.

Marking down individual clearance or special purchase products is fine. These special bargains really fire up your customers.

12 Special nights

Inviting selected customers to join you in the store for an exclusive evening of demonstrations and offers can be very effective. Provide refreshments and snacks and, if appropriate, bring in a relevant speaker, and entertainment too. Try to pick a theme or a special reason for doing it because that can help you to promote the night more effectively. A sports shop, for example, could invite customers in to celebrate Sven-Göran Eriksson's birthday. It's frivolous, sure, but gives you a hook too. This is another one that can get you coverage in the local paper.

13 Surveys

You should be asking customers for their views anyway but surveys can also be used as promotional tools. Create a survey and then mail it to members of your database. Include a 'thank you' voucher for a discount in-store. It reminds customers you are there, it tells them customer satisfaction is important to you and it gives them a reason to come and shop with you.

14 Celebrity visit

Getting a celebrity into your store for a PA (public appearance) can be fantastic for generating traffic. They are not always as expensive as you might think either: TV actors, especially if they live locally, can be a bargain! You can find the contact details of almost all British-based actors in a book called *Spotlight*. Your town library will have a copy. Make sure you tell customers and the local paper that this is happening.

15 Book signings

You don't have to be a bookshop to hold book signings. A fishing tackle shop can get just as much benefit from having the captain of the British Coarse Fishing Team in to sign his new book. In fact it's sometimes a good way for a non-bookseller to get a celebrity in without having to pay them. Heavily promoting the event is key to making a book signing really work for you.

16 Lunch at the store

People are so busy today that lunchtime often becomes a trade-off between eating or shopping. Another idea from the US is to help your customers to do both. Think about putting on a simple lunch for every customer who visits you on one day or one week of lunchtimes. No need for caterers – just open packaged food. Obviously it's worth avoiding foods that are greasy or likely to stain. Leafleting local offices is the best way to promote these events. Word is that they are really very effective at getting new people into your store.

17 Seminars, 'how to's, and in-store events

Absolutely essential whatever your business. Get local traders, designers, and even manufacturers' reps in to show off your products and demonstrate what to do with them. Construct a series of seminars, 'how to' and in-store events and then give every customer a calendar with these marked on it. Seminars attract customers and help them decide to spend more money. 'How to' demonstrations and events such as fashion shows bring theatre and drama into your store. That excites customers and helps to make their experience of your store a much more enjoyable and interesting one.

Seminars attract customers and help them decide to spend more money.

18 Meeting place

If you have a training room or large office that is not fully utilised, consider offering it to local businesses as an outside meeting space. This creates massive goodwill and hardly anyone currently does it, which will mean you will stand out. Maybe invest in a coffee-maker, cups and a lick of paint too to make the place attractive. Check your insurance terms as well just in case.

19 Charity giving

An honest charity promotion is a winner in many sectors. It works especially well if you have an older customer base: mature customers tend to be the most receptive to support of a charity. The usual format would be to partner a particular charity and then agree to donate a stated percentage of profits earned during a specific special charity day.

20 Local radio outside broadcasts

If you have got the space offer to let the local radio station come and do an OB (outside broadcast) from your car park or store. Make it coincide with a strong event and you'll find the station quite keen to be involved.

21 Banded product

This is a cousin of the buy-one get-one free offers. Banding is usually applied to fast-moving lines and involves either attaching a different product to another for free, or putting two products together as a package deal. It's a good way to move a slower line out with a more popular one and to please the customer at the same time.

22 Discount off future purchase

I am a big fan of this technique, sometimes called delayed discount. Every customer buying on the promotional day gets a money-off voucher that they can use in the store on another day. Usually the value of the voucher depends on the value of the original spend, so a typical offer might look like this:

▶ Spend £20 get a £5 voucher off next purchase.

▶ Spend £50 get a £12 voucher.

▶ Spend £100 get a £30 voucher.

You can afford to be quite generous because a high proportion of the vouchers you give out will never be redeemed. Incidentally, make sure that whatever you use is secure and that it has an expiry date and a 0.0001p cash equivalent mark on it.

Promote it on the day with lots of bold signs and make sure you have told all your database contacts to come visit. This promotion type makes a great story for advertising too.

23 Gift certificate promotions

Very similar to the discount off future purchase offer, except redeemed using normal store gift certificates which can be used at any time.

Customers treat gift certificates more like money so redemption rates, and cost too, will be much higher.

24 Buy now pay later

A credit product based promotion. Very popular among big-ticket retailers because it enables customers to fulfil tomorrow's desires today! Actually they are a good deal for both punter and retailer. These promotions don't carry perhaps the same excitement and call to action that they once did – customers are used to seeing them now.

25 Interest-free credit

A very powerful promotion that enables customers to buy your product and pay for it in instalments without them incurring any credit interest. Various deals are available to suit independent retailers and are worth serious consideration if you are aiming to move big-ticket items.

26 Storecards

Storecards earn us retailers a lot of money, and they can be very convenient for some customers. I struggle with storecards though from an ethical standpoint. They are a very expensive form of credit, charging interest rates way above ordinary credit cards or personal loans. Lots of good ordinary people – our customers – get caught out by storecards and run up huge debts with awful consequences. Retail is a people business: I don't believe we should be responsible for making anyone's life more difficult. So for that reason I cannot recommend running a storecard.

27 Bargains

And finally, the most powerful promotion of all: the humble bargain. Customers love bargains. So much so that I have filled this book with thoughts on how to get hold of, promote and sell bargains in your store. Scour your price lists, badger your suppliers, pester

Bargains bring people in, they make them spend more and they bring them back again.

the marketing team, gather up end-of-line or last season stock and go mental for your customers. Bargains bring people in, they make them spend more and they bring them back again.

Promotions planner

Putting together a promotions planner is simple but essential:

1   Start with 12 sheets of A4, one for each month of the year.

2   Write in all the things you can predict will be happening, for example a January sale.

3   Then write down all the predictable quiet times for your business – summer holidays might be one.

4   Then write in all the predictable mad times such as Christmas.

5   Add any product launches that you know of.

6   Write in any major events that could offer some good promotion links – the Olympics or a blockbuster movie perhaps.

7   Now you will have a good idea where you have either dead zones to fill or mad times to avoid or to strengthen. You can also see where some themed promotions might work well.

Choosing the right promotions is an art but this information can really help you. For example, if your business is quiet during August because of summer holidays (when most people are away), it might be sensible to run promotions that maximise transaction values then, and pull more cash in from the few customers you do have.

You can easily use a form of these planners to impress your potential new bosses at interviews too.

Table 11.1 Promotions and the rules of performance improvement at a glance

	1 Sell to new customers	2 Sell more in each transaction	3 Persuade customers to return to your store more often	4 Cuts overheads and improves sales quality
The scale runs 0 to 10: **0 = No effect, 5 = Neutral effect, 10 = Very powerful effect**				
1 Joint activity	7	3	1	8
2 Displays in empty stores	5	0	5	8
3 Sponsorship and town events	4	0	10	4
4 Adverts in changing rooms	0	10	6	6
5 Children's competitions	0	5	7	5
6 Tip sheets	8	6	8	9
7 Loyalty programmes	0	5	10	3
8 Customer-get-customer	8	5	6	5
9 Buy one get one free	8	7	10	2
10 Sampler clubs	1	5	10	7
11 Percentage off	6	7	6	3
12 Special nights	6	7	7	5
13 Surveys	6	0	8	6
14 Celebrity visit	10	0 or 10*	8	2
15 Book signings	8	0 or 10*	8	8
16 Lunch at the store	7	0	8	5
17 Seminars and 'how to' events	8	10	10	6
18 Meeting place	7	0	8	6
19 Charity giving	6	0	6	3
20 Local radio outside broadcasts	6	0	6	8
21 Banded product	8	5	8	7
22 Discount off future purchase	7	7	10	5
23 Gift certificate promotions	8	5	10	5
24 Buy now pay later	7	5	7	4
25 Interest free credit	8	6	8	5
26 Storecards	2	8	7	10
27 Bargains	10	10	10	5

* A celebrity or author who is an expert in the same field as the store can lead customers into buying all sorts of extras to go with a base purchase, a non-related one can't!

12

Marketing for real people

'Tell me what it is, why I'd want one and how to get it. That's all I give a monkey's about. If you can do that in a humorous, dramatic or otherwise attention grabbing way then fine; knock yourself out. Please don't talk to me in Latin, black and white, obtuse images or stuff that goes way over my head because I just don't care enough about you or your product to bother trying to understand your clever rubbish.'

In that one paragraph you have all the rules of advertising you will ever need. Be clear, tell people what the benefit to them is and then make it very easy for them to buy from you. Ad agencies argue that advertising is about building brands too. There is some truth in this, but frankly brand is built more powerfully by your shop, your people in it and your store culture. Slick, eye-candy advertising is simply not important.

easyJet and Richer Sounds have two of the ugliest logos I have ever seen but it makes not one tiny bit of difference. easyJet do cheap flights with no fuss: people fly with them because getting a packet of peanuts and paying twice as much to some other airline is daft. To make it easy for people to book with easyJet their telephone number is painted in five-foot-high letters on the side of their aeroplanes. Punters buy cheap, honest hi-fi from Richer Sounds: the shop never rips customers off, they seem pleased to help people make decisions, and they give customers a catalogue with a list of their stores on.

Both brands tell you what they are for, why you would want to use them and how to do business with them. Both those brands are sales phenomena. Both are never going to win awards for the glossiness of their advertising.

Advertising made simple

Media commentator Charlie Brooker wrote in his *Guardian* blog: '*Marketing is the art of associating products with ideas to bamboozle consumers. People in marketing often talk about the "personality" of a given product. A biscuit might be "reassuring and sensual"; a brand of shoe may exhibit "anarchic yet inquisitive" tendencies. Marketeers have built their worldview on such thinking, despite it being precisely the sort of babble a madman might come up with following years alone in an isolated cottage, during which time he falls in love with a fork and decides the lightbulbs are conspiring against him.*'

When McDonalds slashed their UK advertising budgets they demanded that agencies still deliver just as many 'spots' on TV, radio and posters. The only way this could be done was to cut production budgets. It forced agencies to focus on the 'this is a hamburger, they taste nice, come and buy one' aspects of the brand. McDonalds adverts have never been so effective. So much so that McDonalds have retained this policy for, well, years now. It's an interesting slice of common sense in a crazy branded world.

Beauty has its place

There is space for the beautiful – those breathtaking adverts that force their way into your awareness. But these are very much the exception that proves the rule: you remember them because they are exceptional. Orange, the mobile phone network, has built a hugely successful brand without ever showing a picture of a telephone in its advertising (there was one once when Motorola were paying and forced the issue, but even then the phone featured was only shown as an X-ray). You might think this goes against the simple doctrine I've outlined here. It doesn't. Orange's adverts always tell you what they are for (mobile communications), they always focus on one clearly defined benefit at a time (say the joy of swapping pictures on a mobile) and then they put a great big phone number up onscreen and suggest that interested punters might like to ring it to become an Orange customer.

Marketing things to make and do

Marketing is not a mythical black art. It is nothing more, or less, than a common sense framework: a framework into which adverts and promotions can be fitted. Marketing theory is actually very simple. The skill, especially in the case of retail, is not in cleverly executing the practice of marketing, but in trusting your gut feel to keep things simple. Marketing is about understanding who your customers are, where they can be found, what they want and how much they will pay to satisfy those wants. That's really kind of it.

The four 'P's

One of the basics of marketing theory is a simple concept called the four 'P's. It is very basic but still useful. Here they are:

▶ **Product** – what are we selling?

▶ **Place** – where will it be sold, how will we get it there?

▶ **Promotion** – how will the product or brand be positioned and promoted in the market?

▶ **Price** – how much is the product?

The four 'P's set up a series of questions: Who are we selling to? How do we tell them about our product? What will they pay for it? Notice the way these questions form a chain. The answer to the first informs the second, which in turn sets up the third and so on. Answering these questions can help you to make better decisions on promotions and on advertising.

Questions chain

1   Who wants to shop at a store like mine?

2   What is it they like about us?

3   Which products excite them?

4 What promotions do they like?

5 Where can I find these people?

6 What should I tell them?

You might want to go through these questions in a team meeting. Try to cover four or five main customer types separately. Each customer type looked at will create a slightly different thread. Use what you learn to select target audiences and to select the promotions you would like to put before them. The following pages list some of your options for reaching those audiences.

Reaching customers

Radio

Radio is a great medium. It's very cost effective and you can paint any image you want with words. Often, big and shouty words work best. Plenty of stations will help you to create your advert. Each station will also be able to give you profiles of their listeners for each of their shows. This means you can choose to advertise only on those stations, and only during those shows listened to by people who might actually want to shop with you. There are also lots of resources available for do-it-yourself radio advertisers and that helps makes the medium very attractive.

The Radio Advertising Bureau (RAB) exists 'to guide national advertisers and their agencies towards effective advertising on commercial radio'. They won't be able to advise you directly but their website is a fantastic mine of resources. Click on the truly heroic radio advert archive; all the inspiration you could ever want is there. RAB's address is www.rab.co.uk.

TV

TV is undoubtedly a powerful advertising channel, but it's expensive and it suffers a tendency to have a somewhat scattergun effect. Unless you can afford to advertise on TV lots then it's unlikely that you will reach enough of your potential customers to make this medium pay. The Advertising

Association, www.adassoc.org.uk, has some useful research on its site that you might want to take a look at if you're considering TV. The channels themselves do offer advice and assistance to smaller advertisers so it is worth asking about those services. Ask too about related discounted advertising packages.

Print

Clear, bold messages work best – buy the largest portrait spot you can afford. Don't do national if you are local. Don't be seduced by glamorous graphics. A bold typographical treatment highlighting a great promotion accompanied by a shot of your product is more effective.

Posters

Traditional large-format posters can act like a second storefront but they are expensive. These days anything that doesn't move seems to be available for placing an advert on; everything from posters in pub toilets to the handles of petrol pumps. Maiden is the largest independent outdoor media owner in the UK and worth talking to if you are interested in exploring posters. Their web address is www.maiden.co.uk.

Catalogues

A catalogue can be a single flyer or a 32-page colour extravaganza. Never underestimate the power of catalogues. They provide you with huge scope to tell people about your fantastic deals, and at the same **Never underestimate the power of catalogues.** time talk about why your store is a nice place to visit and to do business with. George Whalin, one of America's most effective retail consultants, suggests that 'if you have one item and just one page, that's a catalogue; start from there and build it over time'.

Catalogues are exciting because there is so much you can do with them. You can hand them out as flyers, you can put them into the local free papers, you can mail them to your customer database and you can give them out to visitors to your store.

Getting them out there

Consider how you might distribute your catalogue. Piles in the store are fine; a stand outside is better. Having a colleague hand them out on the car park or up and down the street is always worth doing. Paying a delivery person to distribute catalogues door-to-door is useful too. Of course this is also dependent on the type of catalogue you have gone for. If yours is thick, heavy and expensive then distribution will have to be more limited. Similarly, if you know that your customer falls into a very narrow interest group then you should consider distributing your catalogue directly to them. For example, a baby goods store might want to have its catalogue in the waiting area of the local maternity ward.

Easy ABC database marketing

Every store can, and must, build a customer database. Used sensibly they drive customers into your store like no other advertising tool can. You don't need complex software or high-powered PCs to run them: any database programme, such as Microsoft's Access, will do. You can even get by fine using just the contacts bit of the free programme Outlook Express (again available from Microsoft). A card index will suffice in high-ticket selling situations where you are servicing a small number of prospective customers.

The best email marketing

How to do email database marketing really well:

1   Always get permission – customers hate email spam, it irritates them. They respond much better to expected messages, so long as these are relevant.

2   Make sure you actually have something to say, for example:

   ▶   exclusive offer

   ▶   hard-to-get item here in stock now

   ▶   end of line special bargain

   ▶   one-off event

► exciting new line due in on X date.

3 Start the email with all your headings, just titles with no additional body text. For example:

► Buy one get one free on all paperback fiction this weekend only.

► New Harry Potter book arrives in-store here on 21 July – reserve your copy now.

► David Beckham here signing his new autobiography on 1 July.

4 Remember, time limits on offers always help to drive customers into action.

5 Then in the body of the email, below these headlines, you can expand on each subject. Try to keep words to a minimum; just tell the story and then get out.

► Buy one get one free on all paperback fiction this weekend only.

► Choose any two from our huge range of great titles and you get the cheapest free. That includes all of our current bestsellers as well as the full selection of classic fiction. Saturday and Sunday only; we're looking forward to seeing you!

6 Remember, close with details of your store including telephone numbers and opening times.

7 Sign it! Customers appreciate a personal touch.

8 Remember the rules: 'Tell me what it is, tell me why I might want one, tell me how to get it.'

The Data Protection Act

If you are going to hold customers' data in a database you must comply with the Data Protection Act. Many retailers have already notified that they wish to be registered under the Act. If you have done so you are likely to be entitled to also use the data you hold for database marketing purposes. You must check though before moving on. If you are in a chain-store branch the company may well have sent notification too but it can be tricky to find out. If you are lucky the marketing team will find out for you and will help you with the small number of compliance issues involved. If you are less lucky and the marketing team get all stroppy then it may be worth considering notifying in the name of your individual store instead. Lots of clear advice on the whole process can be found at www.dataprotection.gov.uk/dpr/dpdoc.nsf.

One of the key aspects of the Data Protection Act is permission. When you ask for someone's details you must tell them that you will be holding these details in a database. You must also get their permission to send them things. Check on the www.dataprotection.gov.uk site for the latest advice on what to say and how to say it. Getting permission is good practice anyway: there is little point in taking someone's address only to send them things they don't want to see.

Postcards

Email is the nice, easy and cheap way to begin database marketing. There is an excellent print alternative though that is still cost effective, especially as a tool for announcing big promotions, sales or for inviting customers to store events. Stores in the US use postcard marketing campaigns very effectively.

Email is the nice, easy and cheap way to begin database marketing.

The usual format is a large postcard where one side is given over to a full-colour image and the other is split into two halves. One of those halves is a space to put an address label and a stamp. The other will usually carry a coupon of some sort.

Local printers are plentiful so get three price quotes and ask to see samples. Get a fixed-cost quote and some examples. Make sure you and the printer both understand exactly what it is that you want. Short print runs are ideal as this lets you send lots of different messages to individual targeted groups of customers over time.

Selecting prospects to send your cards to needs a bit of thought. You want to avoid wastage and to maximise your chances of success. All current and recent customers who could conceivably need to visit you again should be targeted. Think carefully though: writing to someone who bought a sofa from you last week to tell them you are offering 10 per cent off sofas this week is always going to be a bad idea.

Think about your customers. Do groups of them have particular things in common? Do you find yourself selling to people who all live in certain areas of town? Are your products related to their hobbies, or to their work? Are there any age groups that you seem to attract disproportionately? Looking at these factors will help you to identify other groups of people who are not your customers yet but who are very much like your existing ones. These prospect groups are almost certainly worth talking to and a postcard offer might just do the trick.

Case study 12.1 *Smart Retail*: Postcards and the 20 per cent

'Whenever we run a campaign and promote it using postcards, our sales go up 20 per cent.' Andrea Cohen runs young retail business number 35, based in Highgate. She's been successfully trading one store for sometime now and is all set for expanding the brand as a chain. Like a lot of new retailers, number 35 has begun life located slightly off-pitch, in this case a secondary street off Highgate's main shopping area. That means the store has to work harder to gain a foothold in customers' minds. The shop sells a unique product – its own collection of women's clothes tailored to modern shapes (apparently women are that bit more curved in 2007 than they were when most clothes brands cut their patterns). The clothes are great and customer feedback is stunning – for some, number 35's clothes are the answer to a heartfelt prayer. See for yourself at www.no35.co.uk.

The other challenge Andrea has is that these are clothes made to fit the real shape of modern women, but some customers confuse that with 'outsize', when actually the range focuses on sizes 8 to 16. So they are normal sizes but cut to fit really well. It's a message that needs that tiny bit of explanation and postcard promotions fit the bill nicely. So Andrea's technique has been to create a year's-worth of promotions and events and then to drop postcards, via a local newspaper, to support them. The effect is interesting: although the promotional items themselves often only sell in low numbers, reminding customers that the store exists and telling them what the big idea is has the effect of raising overall revenue significantly after each one.

Source: Andrea Cohen

Andrea and the first number 35 store

Keeping track – measurement

Any direct activity needs to be made measurable. You can do this easily by adding coded coupons to printed materials, and by asking email customers to quote a reference code when they come in. It doesn't matter if the customer cannot remember the code, just that they tell you they want to take up an offer you emailed to them.

Set up a basic Microsoft Excel spreadsheet to make tracking easy. Literally just a few columns for the dates and then a few rows for the various promotions you are running. Then record the number of people responding, the total value of their purchases and the margin earned on each transaction. At the end of each week work out the total profit accounted for by your promotions. Then deduct from that the cost of the activity you ran. So long as you capture every relevant sale then this is a crude but perfectly acceptable way to track how well each promotion is working for you.

You also need to take account of the discounts you gave to normal customers; people who would have bought from you regardless of the promotion. That is quite tricky and will often be down to your instinctive judgement. All the same, it is important because this number helps you to realistically appraise returns from your efforts.

13

A brief history of retail

Why things are the way they are

Righty ho – I'm going to take us through the early years, up to somewhere around the 1950s. There are two reasons for doing that – the first is to prove a really important point: retailing is not about inventing new stuff.

Eh? 'But you've gone on and on about ideas being the lifeblood of retailing and that ...'

That's true, I have. Here's the thing: ideas are of course vital but ideas are about change, improvement and development, and rarely about coming up with things that no human has ever thought about before. You can be an innovative retailer by improving on existing ideas, by combining exisiting practices in radical new ways. But you don't have to magically pluck brand new 'things' out of nowhere to be innovative and successful.

And this is a good thing. I'm going to show you over the course of this chapter that there have only really been four important inventions in retailing over the last 2,200 years. This should be liberating for you – in effect, what I'm saying is that you don't have to reinvent the wheel to be innovative.

The four great inventions in retail are:

- *c.* 200 BC – the creation of the first chain of stores (China)
- 17th century – catalogue-based mail order (Europe)
- 1852 – the first true 'department' store (France)
- 1915/16 – self-service (US).

That's it. Yeah, maybe we're overdue something else earth-shattering and new sometime soon, maybe it'll be you that invents it but if not – that's okay! It's not vital to your success as a retailer. Oh, and if anyone is shouting 'Idiot! Hammond's missed out the Internet', calm yourselves down: the Internet is just a development of catalogue-based mail order and don't kid yourself that it isn't.

On that point, right here in St Albans where I'm happily typing away, there's an excellent 19th century analogue to the current thinking among leading Internet players around becoming bricks and mortar retailers. On our original high street there's a beautiful, white, glass, brick and iron-frame building. It looks like a cross between a massive greenhouse and some Victorian baths. Actually, it was built more than a hundred years ago as a showroom for the leading mail-order seed catalogue of the time. It was a place where the seeds could be shown off as plants, where arrange-ments of flowers, trees and shrubs could be suggested to customers and in which expert growers could pass on their tips. Isn't that wonderful? You see – our retail past informs our retail present. The seed showroom is a Café Rouge now. Not sure what that says about the future of amazon.com!

Oh and in the introduction I said there were two reasons for giving you a bit of retail history: the first is to give you the reassurance that you're not trying to invent something nobody has thought of before. The second is to show you that the challenges you face have all been solved before and that you can learn from those earlier experiences.

Actually, there's a third, and perhaps more personal, reason for pulling together this brief history – it's that I believe retail is important and that the heroes of retail should be celebrated and their accomplishments enjoyed as we carve out our own retail successes.

The really early days

So, to the history: the retail trade predates money – money having initially grown out of the need to mark retail debt in a consistent manner. What you do really is one of the oldest professions. It began when man occasionally found that he had a surplus of produce from his efforts to grow food. Once he, his family and his community needs were satisfied then he would attempt to trade his produce for different items he needed. That's the fundamental starting point for retailing.

What you do really is one of the oldest professions.

Markets

Early efforts to trade goods developed into markets. Within a community, specialist skills developed – one producer who had a skill, say in stone implements, would deliberately over-produce so that he could swap his spares for food or clothing with specialists in those areas. All very lovely and old-age, or new-age or something.

Merchants

Two different types of retailer were clearly defined even this early on: the peddlers and the producers. Peddlers were generally a chancy bunch and would purchase any goods that they thought they could sell for a profit. Producers, still selling direct, were interested in selling only the goods that they had themselves produced.

This division continues to this day, although the peddlers have split into two distinct groups: general stores and specialist stores. Examples of the direct-to-customer producer–retailer are now scarce – petrol retail is the best example of a producer selling its goods direct to consumers these days. B&Q, and I mean this in a technical rather than crude sense, is a specialist peddler whereas Tesco could be thought of as the opportunitist general-store equivalent.

The first recognisable shops

Eventually, markets became permanent and took on recognisable form as shops. These shops, along with the logistics required to get the goods to them, were the start of the 'modern' retail trade.

The next stages

Retail chains

That brings us to the concept of the chain-store. It's an interesting evolution – as the markets became more permanent it made sense to construct a logistical infrastructure around those fixed points, and so some of the benefits of the older system of travelling merchants were lost. Successful fixed-location shopkeepers quickly recognised that expanding their square footage (or square cubits or whatever) and growing their potential customer base offered excellent opportunities to make a little more profit. The answer was to open up another shop, and across most ancient cultures these would almost exclusively be operated by a family member. And would you believe, even back then there are records of these fledgling chain-store businesses using their improved volumes to leverage better terms from suppliers.

Popular theory has it that the first significant retail chain was formed in China over 2,200 years ago with a chain of shops owned by a trader called Lo Kass. Though there isn't any solid historical record to definitely beat old Lo Kass's pre-eminence, there is a strong chance that chains existed in Roman times: excavations, across the Empire, have shown that shops there were extraordinarily like small shops today and that there were excellent formal government, commercial and transport infrastructures present even early-on in the Roman period. But nobody thought to write about them, so Lo Kass sort of wins by default.

Limitations

Two things held back the small chains from making the leap to vast multiple retailers – the lack of non-family trustworthy workers and audit systems to keep them so, and the lack of long-distance mechanised travel. It wasn't until the Industrial Revolution, in the 19th century, that chains became much bigger and more widespread. A few of those pioneer chains still exist today.

Places of retail

Generally, retailing has always taken place at the heart of communities. Markets were central points in villages, and inside the largest cities markets would spring up centred on shared-interest locations – animal markets in one quarter, grain in another, cloth elsewhere and so on.

High streets, US-style suburban strip-malls and indoor town-centre shopping malls (or arcades, or centres) are the direct descendants of those community markets. The one major, late 20th century change to retail location history is the out-of-town shopping mall and the edge-of-town retail parks – we'll look at those a little more in a moment.

First I want to get all historical on the development of indoor town-centre shopping – mostly because this *feels* like a modern thing but actually it's a retail idea that goes back more than 1,000 years: Isfahan's Grand Bazaar, which is largely covered, dates from the 10th century AD. Tehran's covered Grand Bazaar, which is 10 kilometres long, also has a very old history. Early Western mall-style arcades include the Burlington Arcade in London, opened in 1819. The Arcade in Providence, Rhode Island introduced the concept to the United States in 1828. The larger Galleria Vittorio Emanuele II in Milan followed in the 1860s.

The move away from high streets

Suburban living, commuting and the rise of the road and car has given birth to what might still come to pass as having been a curiously 20th century phenomenon: the move away from shopping on high streets. Throughout the 1990s, especially in the US, the centre of retail has moved from the old high streets and into giant regional shopping malls and massive stores located in retail parks on the edge of towns.

Lack of space has, to an extent, halted this move in western Europe but even in spacious North America something interesting is happening – high streets are thriving once more. Indeed high street rents in the US are increasing at an astonishing rate: in 2007 it cost 12 times as much to rent a high-street store in an average small American town as it did for the same unit 15 years earlier. Rents tend to mirror commercial success so are a useful barometer of location health. In the UK, high street rents increased 25 per cent in the 18 months to November 2004 and have continued to climb at a furious rate ever since.

It would appear that there is something fundamental about humans and shopping, and doing this within our communities (however superficial those communities may be). I believe that it is only the true destination stores – large furnishings, supermarkets, large electricals and specialist heavy or occasional project-related formats – who will ultimately survive out of town. Fashion, food, entertainment, small specialist, personal technology, personal services and gift retailers will thrive again at the centre of our communities and on our high streets: the added value of convenience, immediacy and shopping in mixed, varied and stimulating locations is rising.

Although the acceleration point, and I believe apex too, lies in the 1990s, the first out-of-town shopping can be traced back to 1950 and the Northgate Shopping Center in north Seattle in the US. Austrian migrant Victor Gruen brought with him ideas formed from his experiences of the inner city shopping district of Vienna. Northgate was an instant hit enabling Gruen, a true retail pioneer, to take his concept further afield. He built the Northland Shopping Center near Detroit in 1954, and the Southdale Center, located in the Twin Cities suburb of Edina, Minnesota, in 1956.

The megamalls

The title of the largest enclosed shopping mall was held by the West Edmonton Mall in Edmonton, Canada for 20 years. The most visited shopping mall in the world and largest mall in the United States is the Mall of America, located near the Twin Cities in Bloomington, Minnesota.

However, several Asian malls are advertised as having more visitors, including Berjaya Times Square.

Department stores

The development of department stores is important because it marks the first real, systematic use of retail theatre – and it's that theatre that has driven almost every single customer-facing innovation since. It is the absolute key component of modern format-planning and concept development. It is what sorts the mediocre from the fantastic.

Until 1852 shops were all small and specialist. That changed forever when Astride Boucicaut and his wife Marguerite expanded their Parisian drapery store and began to also sell housewares and bedlinen. They called their store Bon Marché and its inception marked the arrival of the world's first department store. The store was launched on the back of innovations such as the promise to deliver 'to homes as far as a horse can travel in Paris', and for the first time anywhere the store featured prices clearly written on all labels. The Boucicauts are even credited with the invention of modern stock management, where rotating merchandise and the staging of summer sales, winter sales and blue-cross sales created constant change and excitement in the store.

Then in 1869 Bon Marché moved into stunning new purpose-built premises in the Rue de Sèvres, designed in part by Gustave Eiffel. Imagine how you might have felt the first time you walked through the huge iron and glass doors and into the fabulous interior. Just imagine that thrill: stunning clothes, awe-inspiring furniture, drapery from all corners of the Earth, sweets like you've never seen before, foodstuffs to make the mind boggle and baffling new gadgets you cannot begin to fathom. You see assistants bustling here and there, catwalk displays of clothes and dressed mannequins among showmen demonstrating the latest wonder. Every turn holds something new, a surprise, a wondrous assault to the senses. Imagine too how amazing it felt as you discovered that every department, as well as showing you awesome delights you never knew existed, had lots of nice things in them that you could afford. Bon Marché changed its ranges constantly, and new surprises were guaranteed all the time. It's a

Source: Royal Institute of British Architects Picture Archives

The Grands Magasins du Bon Marché: photograph taken in 1928

product mix and stock management philosophy that worked then and still holds true today.

The concept of browsing a store was alien to the masses before 1852. It just was not a part of the contemporary ritual of shopping. Today browsers are essential to everyone from Wal-Mart through to Harrods.

That's why we pack our stores with hot spots and why we change things so often. It's all down to Bon Marché and their astonishing 19th century Parisian innovations.

The concept of browsing a store was alien to the masses before 1852.

Well, that's not entirely true. One other major, seismic earthquake of change needed to happen and that was the development of self-service shopping. The established retail model, even within multi-department stores such as Bon Marché, was to keep products in cases, behind counters or under glass – customers would be served by an assistant who would fetch customers' products for them.

Self-service

Everything changed in 1915 when Albert Gerrard opened the Groceteria in Los Angeles – the first self-service store. The early part of the 20th century was an extraordinarily competitive time in general-store retail in the US, but even in that white-heat environment it took almost a year for another operator to copy the idea. And what a copy it was! Clarence Saunders, the founder of Tennessee-based Piggly Wiggly, built an entire business around self-service and then, the sly fellow, went and secured a patent on the concept (I've not been able to discover if that patent was ever enforced – I quite enjoy the thought of one of his long-lost relatives appearing out of the woodwork and suing us all, every last retailer on the planet, for a licence fee).

Saunders was something of a legendary loon and had begun construction of a pink marble mansion in Memphis, Tennessee when in 1932 the 'bears' of Wall Street allegedly took him for a million dollars and rendered him personally bankrupt. The 'Pink Palace' is now a museum, and it includes a walk-through model of the first Piggly-Wiggly store, complete with 2¢ packets of Kellogg's Cornflakes and 8¢ cans of Campbell's soup. It's well worth a visit – the place shows you what a real retail innovation actually looks like.

And that's where I'm going to leave the history for now and move on instead to the stories of some of the most important pioneers of our trade.

Source: US Patent Office

Self-service as shown in Saunders' patent grant no: 1,242,872

The pioneers

Say hello to the retail kings – these chaps are the true pioneers of your trade. They had no maps, instead forging their own routes through opportunity and adversity alike. There are a couple of sad endings mind you, so be prepared for that.

George Hartford and George Gilman – A&P (US)

The Great Atlantic and Pacific Tea Company, better known as A&P, is the original American supermarket chain. The company was founded by George Hartford and George Gilman. By 1876 A&P had 67 stores, increasing to 1,000 by 1915. In the 1920s and 1930s, the company utterly dominated the American retail market and by the end of that period A&P was operating approximately 16,000 stores with combined revenue of $1 billion. That power led to the US Congress passing several anti-predatory pricing laws – it's interesting to see similar pressure on goverments today to act in a similar manner in order to curb the practices of some of our most powerful supermarket chains.

That 1930s high has now, to a large extent, evaporated – A&P still trades today but from far fewer locations and it is now far from being the biggest retailer in the US.

In 1859 Gilman opened The Great American Tea Company, a corner shop, on Vesey Street in Lower Manhattan (the site today of Ground Zero). The shop sold teas, coffees, spices, baking powder, condensed milk – all products that often came to America as ballast in the holds of clipper ships. Already you should be seeing parallels with the opportunistic peddlers of the distant past! The name change came in the 1870s when the company began to ship goods via the trans-continental railroad – with their broadened horizons, connecting 'Atlantic' and 'Pacific' must have seemed like an extraordinary achievement.

What marks out Hartford and Gilman from other retailers of the time is their voracious expansion ambition and achievement. Even today, the vast

Source: A&P Historical Society

A typical small A&P at L'Anse, Michigan in the 1950s

bulk of American retailers remain regionalised but the two Georges fired out those 16,000 nationwide, coast-to-coast stores by 1937.

F.W. Woolworth – Woolworths (US)

Franklin Winfield Woolworth (born April 13 1852, died April 8 1919) was *the* American merchant. Born in Rodman, New York, he was the founder of F.W. Woolworth Company, an operator of discount stores that eventually settled into the big idea of pricing merchandise at five and ten cents. He pioneered the now-common practice of buying merchandise direct from manufacturers and was among the first retailers to fix prices on all items rather than haggle, as was the prevailing tradition. Woolworth was also among the first retailers to recognise the potential in selling mass-produced products. Clever man this Mr Woolworth. He was one of the first retailers to truly understand his customers – he recognised that this business is about consistency, choice and democracy (good stuff, at the right price, for all).

Woolworth grew up on a farm but something sparked the retail bug in him pretty early on and it was while working at a dry-goods store that he had his first great idea. He noticed that leftover items were often priced at five cents and placed on a table to get rid of them, he noted how much customers seemed to appreciate the five cent table and on went a light in his brain . . . Woolworth then borrowed $300 to open his own store in which all items were priced at five cents.

That first store, in Utica, New York opened on February 22 1879, and failed before the end of March. At his second store, in Lancaster, Pennsylvania (opened April 1879) he adjusted the format by expanding the concept to include another range of merchandise priced at ten cents. This second range finally balanced the merchandising and the Lancaster store became a great success. Woolworth and his brother, Charles Sumner Woolworth, solidified the template and then went on to open a large number of their five-and-ten-cent stores.

The concept was widely copied, and five-and-ten-cent stores (also sometimes called five-and-dime stores) were a multiple fixture in American downtowns for the first half of the 20th century, going on to anchor suburban strip-malls in the middle part of the 20th century. The criticisms that the five-and-dime stores drove local merchants out of business are exactly the same criticisms faced by the likes of Wal-Mart and Tesco today.

In 1911, the board chose to incorporate the F.W. Woolworth Company – this created an incredibly strong business uniting 586 stores founded by Woolworth, his brother and those belonging to a number of franchise partners.

Always loving the grand gesture, in 1913 Woolworth built the Woolworth Building in New York City at a cost of $13.5 million (which he paid in cash). At the time, it was the tallest building in the world measuring 792 feet, or 241.4 meters. The Chrysler building, with its craftily constructed spire, robbed Woolworth of that record the same year. Can you imagine the sheer balls of a man prepared to make a statement on the scale of the Woolworth Building? I love that – it's madness but it's wonderful too.

Source: PA Photos

The Woolworth Building in New York

As well as its American success, Woolworths extended across into many other countries and in the 1960s and 1970s in the UK, it was an absolute rock of ordinary life. It provided ordinary families, like mine, with nice things at a very low price. The quality was reliable and the range mind-blowing – some 70,000 different lines by the start of the '80s.

Woolworth died in April 1919 at the age of 66. At the time, his company owned more than 1,000 stores and was a $65 million corporation. Ten years earlier he had opened his first British Woolworths, in Liverpool. He went on to personally open 50 UK stores before his death. Opening them himself, especially given the time it took to travel between the US and the UK back then, showed F.W.'s extraordinary commitment to consistency.

Stunningly, all that's left of the original company, following a mass store-closure in 1997, is the Footlocker chain (originally a Woolworths sub-brand). The UK, South African, German, Kiwi and Australian Woolworths are very, very distant cousins having all been independent of F.W. Woolworth and of each other for decades.

Ingvar Kamprad – IKEA (Sweden)

Ingvar Kamprad was born in Sweden on March 30, 1926 and is the founder of IKEA, having opened the first store in 1943. Not entirely sure why but the earliness of that date surprises me every time I see it. As modern as it feels, IKEA has a long history and it is thoroughly imbued with the benefits of evolution over an nice long time.

Ingvar developed his first business as a lad, selling matches to neighbours from his bicycle. He found that he could buy matches in bulk very cheaply from Stockholm, sell them individually at a low price, and still make a good profit. From matches, he expanded to selling fish, Christmas tree decorations, seeds and later ballpoint pens and pencils. When Ingvar was 17, his father gave him a a little cash for doing well at school. He used this cash to establish what has grown into IKEA.

Early IKEA was very much about opportunist peddling of products, but the big growth came after Kamprad started to think systematically about selling furniture when his guiding philosophy came to be 'A better life everyday for the majority of people'. I think he meant it too: IKEA is about much more than generating profits. It offers good things to lots of people at a low cost and without class distinctions. It is accessible, exciting and honest.

The story of why IKEA customers go into a warehouse area to pick up their furniture is a good illustration of why this company is so great. In the early days of IKEA you didn't do that – a helper went and found your stuff for you. Then in 1965 they opened a big, new store in Stockholm and on the first day, sales went crazy. There were more customers than the store could handle. Things were awful at the collection area. So the store manager made a judgement call, opened up the warehouse and allowed customers to come in and find their own items. It worked so well that they tried it again another day and the rest is history. In IKEA that manager was recognised for having improved the way the store worked. Anywhere else and he'd have been reprimanded for breaking the rules.

In 1976 Kamprad wrote his seminal retail manifesto 'Testament of a Furniture Dealer'. In it you read statements such as 'to make mistakes is

Source: PA Photos

A typical IKEA store

the privilege of the active person. Only while asleep does one make no mistakes' and 'an idea without a price tag is unacceptable'. That character is strong in IKEA all over the world. It is so strong that it can be made to cross cultural borders. IKEA in Croydon is as recognisable in its IKEA-ness as IKEA in Gothenburg. I truly believe IKEA to be the best retail company to have ever opened its doors to a customer – it has become almost the sole source for furnishings for many households across the world.

My single criticism of IKEA is that the company hasn't moved its design forward fast enough.

However, there's a word of caution here too, and that's the risk of ubiquity. There is a backlash beginning to rise against 'IKEA style' in which a home furnished exclusively by IKEA is considered to be a bit naff. My single criticism of IKEA is that the company hasn't moved its design forward fast enough. We've had nearly a decade of the IKEA revolution in the UK and the products seem to be broadly similar now to the early days.

Sam Walton – Wal-Mart (US)

Sam Walton, the founder of Wal-Mart, is a customer genius. More than that, in creating the world's biggest company (not just the biggest retailer) he also showed how to create a consistency of culture that is truly gobsmacking. Every single member of the worldwide Wal-Mart team knows exactly what the company does, how it should do it and why. The stores are packed with bargains, dependable value and lots of things to make customers smile.

This edition of *Smart Retail* is likely to still be around in 2012 and if you're reading it then (er, now?) there is a significant chance that some of Wal-Mart's massive lead will have eroded. The company is facing pressures from homegrown upstarts such as Target, as well as encountering challenges in critical overseas markets (Aldi, for one, drove Wal-Mart out of Germany in 2006). Certainly, some of the 'Sam magic' appears to be slipping away from the company (Walton died in 1992). US employee unrest in particular is fast becoming a serious issue – it needs addressing before it's too late, and before the goodwill that does still broadly exist within the workforce is further eroded.

So, the clouds on the horizon – largely issues after Sam's time – dealt with, let's get back to the good stuff: Sam Walton's great legacy is everyday low pricing. As an early operator of franchised Ben Franklin five-and-dime stores, Walton made the unilateral decision to cut margins to the bone in a drive for volume. He chose everyday products on which to focus his most aggressive price discounting: toothpaste and ladies' pants were among his favourite and most successful choices. The simple observation that it was better to sell a ton of product at low margin than to sell a small volume at a high margin drove the almost unchallenged 60 years of Wal-Mart growth.

Some of Walton's most innovative ideas aren't around promotion or price but relate to his work on cutting costs (savings that he then always passed on to customers). He was the first to offer his store managers a profit-share – essentially he said 'It's your business; manage it as such and you will receive a share in the success'. Walton recognised that this would make his managers focus more on controllable costs, on taking advantage of product opportunities and on reducing shrinkage. Another Walton innovation is the 'greeter' – a member of staff standing in the entrance to stores, welcoming customers in. This system (which was actually introduced first by one of Walton's managers as a temporary thing but recognised by Walton as a valuable permanent practice) dramatically cut customer theft at the same time as making arriving customers feel a little bit more important.

Though price became an absolute obsession for Walton, I don't believe it was ever a greed thing. I'm convinced that driving the focus on price was Sam's heartfelt belief that ordinary people should always get the best possible deal. It was an honest proposition that made him and his family an awful lot of money but that also reduced the cost of everyday items for hard-working honest citizens.

Wal-Mart has always attracted criticism from smaller retailers who accuse the company of exploiting their buying power to drive high-street and local retailers out of business. To an extent that's true and it's why I believe that some measure of government control on monopoly and single-centre retail power is sensible – but that's only half the story. Many, not all but many, of those retailers who go bust in the wake of a Wal-Mart

Source: Bobak Ha'Eri

Sam Walton's original store: now the Wal-Mart Visitor Center, Bentonville, Arkansas

opening are doing so because they fail to offer their customers anything particularly special – there's no added value there. Walton himself challenged small retailers to quit the bellyaching and *'Work out what you can do that we can't and then get really good at that thing and get really good at telling your customers about it.'*

Quite right. That's good advice – get busy living!

The Gordon Selfridge method – Selfridges & Co. (UK)

Harry Gordon Selfridge opened a large store in London's Oxford Street on 15 March 1909 and named it Selfridges (the current store, frontage included, is larger still having been extended sometime later). A clean-living, dedicated man, Selfridge came alive when on the shop-floor – he went from accountant to showman and is the true father of great retail theatre. Indeed the resurgence of the once moribund 1970s Selfridges is entirely down to another great retail entertainer – Vittorio Raddice. The key to Selfridge's early success was his decision to move products out from behind the counters and to make them accessible to customers. He wanted punters to be able to touch, explore and be excited by products (before an assistant then helped the customer to actually make the final selection – true self-service still being six years, and a continent, away).

A key component in the Selfridges format was staff behaviour: he wanted them to be accessible but never aggressive, knowledgeable but never smug. He is the man most often credited with originating the phrase 'The customer is always right' – an edict that permeated throughout the customer experience in-store. To be fair, I'm not sure we really know who first actually said that phrase but Gordon will do for now. Selfridge also recognised that he could make as much money delighting the less well-off as from selling crazy curios to the rich. In this way Selfridges was a democratiser – it was a store that welcomed and treated all customers equally. That simply had not happened before, and is an important lesson in how to spread your appeal without diluting your brand.

Selfridge recognised the power of wonder to drive customer traffic and was always on the hunt for grand opportunities to demonstrate the world's cutting edge. In 1909, after the first cross-Channel flight, Louis Blériot's monoplane was exhibited in the store where it was seen by 12,000 people. The first public demonstration of television was by John Logie Baird from the first floor of Selfridges from 1 to 27 April 1925. Just two examples in a long history – and Raddice brought this sense of occasion back to the store with a series of powerful events and themed months. Of late, these themed events haven't felt quite as creative, passionate or as authentic as they did under Raddice. Selfridges, in the period up to 2005, was the best store in the world but it isn't right now. I hope that changes.

Back to Gordon: he was born in Wisconsin, USA on January 11 1858. In 1879 he joined the retail firm of Field, Leiter and Company (which later became Marshall Field and Company). Over the next 25 years Selfridge worked his way up the commercial ladder. He was appointed a junior partner and made a significant pot of capital for himself as well as successfully helping to manage the business.

VANITY FAIR SUPPLEMENT   MEN OF THE DAY. No. 1308.

"Self —"

(Mr H. Gordon Selfridge)

Source: National Portrait Gallery

The man and his store, *Vanity Fair* 1911

His move to the UK was a huge gamble, really dramatic stuff, and came after he'd taken a holiday in London in 1906. He and Mrs Selfridge had been utterly underwhelmed by the retail offerings there, and over the next few years Selfridge plotted a return: this time as a retailer rather than a customer. In 1909 he came back to London with £400,000 capital and chose to invest it by building his own department store in what was then the unfashionable western end of Oxford Street.

I'm as much fascinated by the man as by his store – he was a great retail entertainer, understood inside and out the importance of surprise, discovery, delight and 'wow' but in his formal business dealings, and in his private life, he was hugely restrained and at all times absolutely professional.

And then, in 1918, Mrs Selfridge died.

Gordon went crackers in the most splendid fashion. First off he began to spend extravagantly, abandoned his teetotal tradition in favour of booze and maintained a busy social life with lavish parties at his home – Lansdowne House in Berkeley Square. He bought Highcliffe Castle in Hampshire and promptly moved in a set of music-hall lovelies – triplet sisters as it goes – and appears to have kept them as handy mistresses. It was almost as if Selfridge had finally given in to his own heady retail dream and decided to let it rule him.

But what goes up and all that: during the years of the Great Depression, Gordon watched his fortune evaporate – not helped by his gambling habit. In 1941 he was forced out of the Selfridges business, moved from his mansion and in 1947 he died in absolute poverty in Putney, south-west London. In his last few years the old man was regularly sighted, in tramp's clothing, outside the Selfridges store – a shocking end to a stunning life.

PART FOUR – **STORE**

Surprise and delight to put more money in the till

Source: MPREIS. Thomas Jantscher http://www.jantscher.ch/web02e/index.cfm

Note: That's a supermarket! Austria's MPREIS chain use hot architects to design every store – each is then unique. They use the very fabric of the store to differentiate their business.

CHAPTER FOURTEEN
Discovery!

All shopping is about discovery. The point at which that discovery is made may shift but no shopping trip is ever made without it. Our role as retailers is to create discovery-based formats and to work out how to best merchandise the store in order to take advantage of discovery.

Point of discovery

Sometimes the discovery will be made 100 per cent before leaving the house, research having been done online, in magazines and among friends. That applies significantly to big-ticket items but even then, having spent years watching actual customer behaviour in-store, perhaps not as often as we might assume.

Brand loyalty, to product brands rather than to retail brands, will also drive a certain amount of prior discovery but even that is disruptable by the right promotion. The vast majority of discovery is done in-store – it happens during the shopping trip and few retailers currently take advantage of this process properly. Those that do find it hugely powerful.

In the first edition I wrote about 'surprise' being incredibly valuable in-store: 'Surprise is about delivering on a customer expectation. What are customers doing when they browse your store? They are subconsciously demanding that you divert their attention. They are crying out for you to put that perfect pair of shoes under their nose. They are insisting that an unmissable recipe leaps out at them. Here's a wonderful thing: Paco Underhill, author of *Why We Buy*, has proved that customers, if they buy anything, almost always buy the first thing they pick up. Surprise makes people touch

Make a customer say 'wow' in your store and you've got a sale. things. Make a customer say "wow" in your store and you've got a sale.' Since then my team and I realised that I'd only identified half the story – that surprise is hugely important but that the real power comes from helping customers to make their discovery. Discovery is not just about showing customers surprising things. It is the more complete process of helping to guide them to the highlights of your range, to the great promotions. It's about using great service to lead customers to the right choices and structuring whole formats to provide moments of discovery throughout the customer journey.

Take a look at the Stew Leonard's case study later: it illustrates exactly what I mean by the difference between discovery and surprise. If you're managing a store within an existing chain it's well worth picking up the principles of discovery and using them to squeeze your store's merchandising to the limits. Try stuff and communicate back everything that works – use this as an opportunity to influence the direction of the business and to raise your personal profile. If you're one of those lucky people in a position to create, adapt or relaunch a format then I urge you to put discovery at the centre of your decisions. Doing so will increase footfall, increase conversion and help your team to maximise average transaction values.

Benefits of leading by discovery

Footfall

A reputation as a store that can meet customers' subconscious desire for discovery will drive your footfall. Customers tend to visit stores that meet their needs – a need for inspiration, surprise and ideas is satisfied in a store that has built discovery into its format and merchandising. At its most simple it's about making yours a store that punters out on a shopping trip feel like they want to drop into 'just because'.

Conversion rate

This is a no-brainer: if you can actively get more of the best parts of your range into the minds and hands of customers as they browse your store then the more often you will convert those browsers into buyers.

Average transaction value

Discovery is also about the total sale – everything a customer might need to get the best out of their purchase. So that might be accessories with an outfit, insurance with a phone, sauces with the pasta. It's also about creating such a credible service position that your people are better able to give customers the right advice on a total package – especially important in big-ticket situations.

Linking principles together

This is still all good, simple stuff – the only hard part is ensuring that there is consistency along through your big idea, mission, values and into the way in which you tackle discovery. It's a little bit 'chicken and egg', but faced with a blank sheet of paper I would make sure that my big idea was something that could be delivered with the techniques of discovery. Mission and values, what the business exists to do and the spirit in which it does it, should then slot into that nicely.

The different types of discovery

There are broadly four approaches to tackling the discovery opportunity: promotion-led, service-led, format-led and product-led. A small handful of retailers, Stew Leonard's included, take advantage of discovery across all four approaches and others combine two, sometimes three. Where I've listed a retailer as a great exponent of a particular approach it's because that's the one at the heart of what they do best.

1. Traditional promotion-led discovery

This is the most common approach and if you're able to offer great deals it's very powerful. The availability of those deals is only half the story though – really high-quality merchandising is the critical component: getting your deals, and the benefits of them, into customers' faces.

Tool kit

▶ Creative promotions
▶ Variety of promotions

Source: Koworld

Be a kid again – get enthused by discovery

▶ A near-guarantee that there will be a deal for every customer, every time

▶ Consistent low prices on core products

▶ A retail type that encourages regular revisit

▶ Celebration of the offers by putting them in good locations and regular inclusion of the 'good stuff'

▶ Store layout that includes plenty of hot-spots

▶ Planned customer journey that leads visitors between those hot-spots.

Tesco – the international blueprint for promotion-led discovery: go walk their floor as an observer and learn how to select, place and promote offers brilliantly.

Play.com – this online UK retailer is a genuine challenger to Amazon in many categories. One of the reasons for this is that Play is significantly better at promotion-led discovery than Amazon: the site works very hard to ensure that relevant deals are always in view and runs regular, well-promoted, aggressively-priced sales that manage to feel like proper bargain events.

B&Q – always good at promotional deals but what puts them into this premier division of promotion-led discovery is their approach to pricing core project items. Let's take decking – the deck planks themselves are almost at give-away prices: only a few pounds for each 3 metre length. A wandering customer will do their initial value calculation – (the one done in your head when you've actually come in for something else) – based on the cost of the decking planks alone. That makes the cost of the project appear to be very low. It is only when adding the cost of frame timbers, posts, screws, joints and finishes that the true project cost emerges. By this point it's a bit academic because you've already pictured yourself out on the deck enjoying a summer barbeque.

Boots – poor old Boots comes in for a lot of stick but I believe it's a fantastic retailer. Boots is really a dreary old chemist, yet customers like to drop in for treats, bargains and gifts. That's a stunning leap out from their core purpose. One of the things Boots does really well that has helped them to make that profitable leap is promotions: they practically own the concept of three-for-two offers and are very good at communicating these offers, displaying them and refreshing them.

2. Service-led discovery

This is all about using your people to provide customers with a fantastic discovery experience. We're talking motivated, well-trained, professional teams encouraged to dedicate themselves to providing the best and most honest advice, suggestions and after-sales service. Keys to achieving this are all written up in the 'team' section of this book – go do that stuff and your customers will love you for it. Love you with their wallets.

Tool kit

▶ Make it clear that you trust your team with your customers: that your number one priority is the satisfaction of both

▶ Treat your people with respect

▶ Offer them great training and lots of it

▶ Allow and enable your people to experience the products you sell: give them big staff discounts and operate loan programmes for new products

▶ Get your people involved in the supply chain: allow them to see how things are sourced and made. Doing so will help them to enthuse about your products and, more importantly, to identify what makes your stuff great

▶ Structure your reward programme such that it is biased towards customer satisfaction and away from sales volumes

▶ Put in place a recognition programme and use it to say 'thank you' each and every time you see your people go the extra mile for customers

▶ Value knowledge highly but also encourage your team to always be open-minded and make sure they understand that every customer has their own set of needs

▶ Stress the value of listening to what customers tell us they need and show how this is more important than telling customers what we assume they should have

The Container Store – they are brilliant at this. They provide phenomenal levels of training, wonderful employment experiences and work incredibly hard to build stable, customer-focused teams. The result is a business that punches well above its weight and that enjoys a near-fanatical level of customer support.

Carphone Warehouse – I get a bit of stick for holding up CPW as an example of great retailing so often but I'm not going to apologise for that. When a retailer is this good, and for all the right reasons, then they need to be singled out. CPW is all about service-led discovery: customers walk into these stores often with nothing more than the notion that they want a new mobile phone. They do so, overwhelmingly, with the prior knowledge that the CPW assistant will honestly, and accurately, discover the right answers to that vague need.

John Lewis Partnership – a by-word for honesty, quality and great customer care in the UK. Customers are drawn to John Lewis because they feel sure that the team there will help them to discover the right stuff for them. JLP has been especially good at doing this in high-ticket electricals and computing – areas perhaps not traditionally associated with the store but where customers appreciate in-store guidance nonetheless.

3. Format-led discovery

There are a number of retailers who have based their entire big idea and formats around discovery and paths to discovery. These are the stores you find full of handwritten notes to you, the customer, recommending products. Everything in the store is about making sure that you are aware of how brilliant product X will be for you, how you will feel, what a difference this thing will make to your health, well-being or lifestyle. Written down, that sounds a bit 'ad-man'. It's worth saying that in order to convince properly, the format must be honest, credible and authentic too. Oh, and this is important: format-led discovery only works if there is service-led discovery in place too.

Tool kit

▶ Create an authentic voice for the brand

▶ Use your values to ensure that voice properly represents your big idea and mission

▶ Create a compelling conversation throughout the customer journey: make use of space on product, bags, shelf-edges, in changing rooms, on product cartons, walls, editorial, at the till and so on

▶ Provide honest advice from written communications through to staff help

▶ Celebrate the great products: be enthusiastic, explain to customers why you think item X is so great

▶ Constantly refresh displays

▶ Get customers involved with recommendations

▶ Make good use of customer advocacy: make it easy for customers to tell others about your store and range

▶ Remember that it's the conversation that's important

▶ Make good use of seasonal and 'occasion' events

Apple Store – these iconic retail bases for Apple's products are entirely about discovery. They are built, ground-up, around the notions of 1) non-Apple people discovering that Apple meets their needs better, and 2) of dedicated Apple users discovering more that they can do with their Apple products. So you have every single part of the Apple range, in quantity, out on the shop-floor set up so customers can touch them, play with them, have fun with them and discover new things with them. Then the Apple Genius team – extremely well-trained customer advisors – make themselves easily available to give advice, recommendations and solutions. In the early days I wondered if the Apple Stores would turn out to be heavily subsidised brand promotion rather than profitable stores. I can't say how I know, but I *can* say that the opposite is true: the stores are very profitable as well as being stunningly successful discovery zones for loyal and new Apple customers alike.

Target – the team here recognised that in order to beat K-Mart and to avoid a Wal-Mart smothering, they would need to offer something different within the variety-store format – and they chose discovery. They did that by building the entire store around innovative displays; by bringing in young and hot designers; through a perfect collaboration with Martha Stewart; and by creating a much friendlier and more open atmosphere than is usual in this type of store. Indeed Wal-Mart have even been forced to create a sub-format to tackle Target on Target's ground. These slightly more upmarket Wal-Marts drop the McDonalds, narrow aisles and guns and replace them with better fixtures, more space and independent café concessions. But without the style and authenticity of Target's 'expect more, pay less' big idea, I'm not sure these new Wal-Mart formats will be as successful as perhaps they need to be.

Pret a Manger – these sandwich shops do authentic conversation better than any other retailer in the world. Should you find yourself reading this book while sitting at one of Pret's stainless-steel counters you would find that the coffee cup you're drinking from has a note on it explaining how Pret's coffee has come to taste as good as it does. That cup would explain too how Pret supports the grower of the beans your coffee was made from. You might then dab the corners of your mouth with a Pret napkin that tells you it's made from unbleached, recycled fibres – explaining why that's a good thing. This conversation Pret a Manger has with its customers is powerful and is about helping customers discover a lunchtime option that meets a deeper set of perceived needs. There's a lot of research evidence which proves that human beings' sense of taste is affected by contextual information – telling somebody that they *should* expect to enjoy their sandwich more because it is fresh increases the likelihood that they will enjoy it more. You can use that in lots of ways in retail – we're generally really bad at communicating emotional or sensual information so directly to our customers.

Firebox – stuff for grown-ups. Lovely. Firebox use the best online techniques to involve customers in recommendations by allowing them to upload honest comments (and note that Firebox allow qualified negative feedback as well as glowing praise – that helps build authenticity), and to create and upload pictures and videos of products in action. The voice Firebox have chosen for the brand is one of 'Hey you lot – this is ace! We love doing this for a job, and everything we've found for you is stuff we like and would happily have at home.' That positioning is carried throughout the site: range integrity is paramount, returns are easy and no-quibble, reviews are honest and fun. This voice is then spread from the website to emails, a brilliant catalogue and to little touches such as free sweets thrown into delivery cases seemingly at random. These communications are brilliant at introducing customers to new things and making sure that everyone gets a chance to discover brilliant stuff.

Lush – the store you smell before you see, has format-led discovery pretty much sewn up. Everywhere you look there are handwritten signs full of humour and passion telling you why they love the stuff they sell. Lush's discovery positioning was born of a big idea that was genuinely new: to create cosmetics from pure fruit and vegetable ingredients with no link, at any stage, to animal testing. Instead of being terribly po-faced about that positioning, the team behind Lush chose instead to have fun. Stores are merchandised in a unique way that sits somewhere between authentic French market-stall, English jumble sale and display stand at an expo. I like it a lot – the method makes it really easy for customers and staff to interact with the product and with each other.

Urban Outfitters – you'll notice that I categorise most fashion stores in the product-led discovery category. Urban Outfitters makes the jump because of the innovative way they have constructed their display systems, the credible addition of non-clothes ranges and the considered inclusion of bought-in ranges at key points in the season. All displays at Urban Outfitters are mix and match – tables, shelves and rails can be easily combined, moved and re-merchandised. This makes it easy for the team to constantly refresh the store and to use a form of convection to bring different items to the surface before allowing these to settle back into main stock as new items then get pulled to the surface.

4. Product-led discovery

The product is the star: innovation, fashion, trends and great iconic design are the critical factors in such stores. So we're talking about the kinds of stores that are great at buying, merchandising and refreshing the ranges. But it's more than that – it's critical that the top team in this sort of store have an innate understanding of the principles and power of design and that they can sense the zeitgeist among their target customer groups. A lot of expensive single-store businesses start up as retail business in this category – and an awful lot of them fail. They fail because the owners mistake 'knowing what I like' with 'knowing what customers want'. When done right though, the approach can be incredibly successful – the very best fashion and furnishings stores are great examples of product-led discovery shops.

Tool kit

▶ It's all about your buying: spotting exceptional products, at the right price-points

▶ Hang on, maybe it's all about your merchandising: showing off those products in inspirational settings?

▶ Study all the sources of information on trends you can find: subscribe to trade-specific designers' magazines such as *Frame* and *Creative Design*

▶ Watch what goes on in competitors' stores very closely: look for clues on trends

▶ Talk to customers, get feedback all the time

▶ Ask customers what's hot and encourage them to make recommendations on new finds and new directions

▶ Investigate design leads

▶ Ensure key products are given room to breathe and are displayed to their absolute best

▶ Be prepared to drop poor-performing lines early (or at least to change emphasis if you can)

▶ Refresh ranges often, but show respect for important classic lines too

▶ Do not presume to dictate taste, but do try hard to influence it

Habitat – it's had its ups and downs but right from Sir Terence Conran's early days launching the business, Habitat has been at the forefront of shaping British living. Habitat sold the duvet to a country raised under scratchy sheets and did it by explaining to us that the duvet represented freedom from domestic chores. They made every 1980s kitchen complete by selling each and every last man, woman and child on the planet a red, yellow, blue or green teapot. They helped my Mum and Dad feel comfortable enough to throw dinner parties by suggesting that a chicken brick, or a pressure cooker, was the secret to a successful entertaining. Mum and Dad divorced in 1988 so I'm blaming Habitat for that too. Following on from a few quiet years the now IKEA-owned Habitat is back in front and once again leading on design-discovery alongside its continued celebration of the classics.

Top Shop – no other fashion store anywhere in the world is as good as Top Shop currently is at product-led discovery. No young British woman, and no hip visitor to the UK, leaves Top Shop out of their shopping trip. The sheer weight of fantastic, right-on-the-money fashion that blitzes through the store and into customers' wardrobes is truly mind-boggling. As the earlier case study on the store suggests, this is almost entirely down to Top Shop's commitment to stocking only brilliant items. Everything they sell works – or it's dropped fast; ranges are refreshed at speed; one-offs come in and go out (and onto eBay) at the blink of an eye; even the celebs like to say they've been in and raided Top Shop. The business is all about making customers feel the urge to come in as often as possible in a bid to discover the best new stuff before anyone else does.

ILVA – yes the comparisons to IKEA are valid and yes the store has struggled in its early UK period, but this team is onto something long term. As more people across Europe grow tired of the IKEA formula, the ILVA approach will become stronger in customers' consciousnesses. What ILVA does so well is to take the IKEA idea but to move it upscale a little in terms of presentation, and to broaden the higher ends of the ranges without compromising the lower. They do this by making key pieces the centre of attention and producing an aspirational display.

Case study 14.1 *Exceptionally Smart Retail*: Stew's not mad . . .

Stew Leonard's is barking. Often literally. Oh and it's baa-ing, moo-ing and clucking too much of the time. Stew's is a chain of just four stores in north east USA that together take $300,000,000 a year. That turn nearly $4,000 per square foot and that achieve revenue-per-employee above $150,000. Staggering, stunning, mind-blowing numbers.

And what is Stew Leonard's? A dairy store.

Yep. They sell a limited selection of 1,000 dairy and dairy-related products – albeit within massive megasites. To 125,000 customers each week.

My publisher isn't keen on me using expletives in the book and here is one of the places in which I'd really, really like to put one. I mean those numbers are just unreal.

And although I suspect current boss Stew Leonard Jr wouldn't call it by this name, discovery is what sits at the heart of the amazing performance of this business. The entire format is built around discovery: loads to see and do and a massive single aisle that snakes customers past every last part of the massive store. Promotion-led discovery is there in spades, and in massive volume. Product-led discovery is particularly important, with what they claim to be the freshest milk in North America bottled on-site in a glassed-in lab visible to all customers. Service-led promotion is also incredibly important: the employment experience at Stew Leonard's is of a very high standard (and regularly recognised as such in *Fortune Magazine*'s annual '100 Best Companies to Work For' list).

The customer is king here and that's literally set in stone – at the entrance to each store there's a three-ton rock carved with these words:

Our Policy

Rule 1
The customer is always right!

Rule 2
If the customer is ever wrong, reread Rule 1.

Stew Leonard

What's critical to the delivery of this policy is that the management team gives every employee a real say in how to best service customer needs. If an employee thinks that doing X is good for the one customer in front of them, they will get on and do it. If they think Y is good for all customers then they will suggest the business gets on and does that too. There is a great story Stew Jr tells that illustrates this in action – he calls it the tuna fish story: 'I unwrap one of our tuna fish sandwiches, and this package of mayonnaise rolls out. I figure the sandwich has enough mayo already. So I call Bill Hollis, my deli manager, and tell him "... get rid of the extra mayo, it's expensive." So next week, I open a sandwich, the mayo rolls out again. I call Bill, and he says "... you gotta talk to Mary Ekstrand, she makes the sandwiches." I call Mary, who says "Sorry, Stew, the customers want the extra mayo, so I'm packing it again." You know my reaction? Bravo, Mary!'

Stew Jr has a cheesy but perfect acronym that illustrates his management style nicely. It's S.T.E.W.: Satisfy the customer; work together as a Team; strive for Excellence in everything you do; and get the customer to say WOW.

That 'wow' thing is a foundation principle of all forms of discovery: it means customers have found stuff that meets that discovery need. The team have created what the *New York Times* calls 'The Disneyland of Dairy Stores', and it is: banjo-playing robot dogs sing Dixie, and animatronic milk cartons (The Farm Fresh Five) dance near a model cow that tells jokes when kids pull its bell. Staff dress as cows, ducks, chickens and bananas while patrolling the aisles giving out free ice-cream and helium balloons. Free food samples are everywhere and staff offer them accompanied by warm, genuine smiles. There are petting zoos, outdoor BBQs, beach grills, cafés and singing broccoli and carrots. Shoppers don't just come here to buy a quart of milk – they come for the experience. An experience built on discovery.

Thing is – this store might feel like it's lots of things just thrown together, but that's not really true. This is a place built by its people. Those 125,000 customers come along each week because they like the products (sure), for the atmosphere (definitely), but mostly I suspect they come because the human experience at Stew Leonard's makes them feel good. That's down to the dedication, imagination and vision not of just one man, but of a whole motivated, passionate team.

CHAPTER FIFTEEN

The great big theatre of shop

One of the most effective lessons in retail can be learned by taking a walk into one of the really hardcore selling environments, where customers are transient and pitches are furious. The two that best illustrate these situations are outdoor markets and a consumer expo.

One of the best of these lessons can be had for free just by walking down the Whitechapel Road at lunchtime. This stretch of East London highway is home to a permanent street market. The traders here compete to sell clothes, food, CDs of questionable authenticity, electronics and homewares. There is even one guy there who sells beds. Six-foot beds, bunk beds, lots of them, on display, on a little market stall!

Take a look at

1 Vocal promotion

2 Merchandising

3 Pricing logic

4 Demonstration.

1 Vocal promotion

Traders calling out to punters can be exhilarating to watch, especially when it's done well. What you can learn from observing is a sense of what really turns customers on. The lines shouted out have been passed down from trader to trader over generations. Traders still use them because they work.

Go beyond the old-time vocal theatricals and you can see some incredible promotional instinct at work. But you don't have to shout – you can let your point of sale (POS) do that for you. Consider how you might transfer some of that into your store POS.

2 Merchandising

When I last walked the Whitechapel Road, lychees were the big popular draw offered by grocers there. The market contains six grocery stalls each offering similar products, although one uses specialism very effectively by featuring a display of hard-to-find Bangladeshi cooking ingredients. It was the merchandising of lychees on these very busy grocery stalls that was so interesting. Lychees were all presented at the front of each stall, right out in the flow of customers. If these were normal high street shops then the lychees would be on the pavement outside the imaginary shop's doors. Each pallet of lychees was presented still stacked on a delivery trolley. At first I thought this was just because the fruits were in the middle of actually being delivered. Next day though the lychees were again right out front on their delivery trolleys.

I asked stallholder Dinesh why he did this: 'It's freshness.' Dinesh said that customers who saw the lychees tended to believe the fruits were really fresh because they hadn't been around long enough to be taken off the delivery trolley. 'How fresh are they?' I asked.

'Three days these ones.'

'Do your customers believe your lychees are fresh every morning?'

'Yeah, they do.'

The story of the lychees illustrates two brilliant merchandising rules

1   Perception is an astonishingly powerful customer motivator.
2   Prominent positioning of hot items hooks customers.

3 Pricing logic

The pricing logic in play on market stalls looks very simple: lots of bargains to attract punters. Actually, each stall has three pricing strands in place:

1   The stunningly cheap, prominently placed 'call birds'. An example might be 'Three T-shirts £4'.

2   Ticket prices – what is shown on the handwritten price tags and signs.

3   Negotiated prices – the price after haggling.

The negotiated price offers an excellent lesson in deal-making. Something more complex than simple haggling is going on. Ask the guy who runs the clothes stall for his cash price on a £15 pair of jeans and his reply isn't '£14 mate' but a much cleverer 'I'll do you two pairs for £25'. Push him a bit further and he might go on to chuck in a free belt too. Instead of just falling over and giving in to your demand for a discount he has ensured that he turns stock around faster and increases his average transaction value. A calculator-like understanding of his margins helps in those on-the-spot deals but you can teach all your staff to do this too.

Demonstration

Demonstration is a phenomenally powerful promotional tool. Watch the stallholders closely. They handle the product constantly: rotating CD titles to the front, shifting clothes, rearranging sizes or colours, juggling sweets, playing music, sparking up toys, cooking up spices on their hot-plates. Almost every grocer you see will actually hold a bag of product in his hand as he barks out the deal on that item. At consumer shows this becomes even more overt where salespeople draw crowds by putting on displays of their product's prowess.

Another great training ground for learning demonstration skills (and I am serious) are the shopping channels on cable and satellite TV. Watch the guest presenters especially. These are the people from the product manu-facturers who get to come onto the show and plug their wares. These men and women are brilliant instinctive performers who talk and demonstrate benefit after benefit. Imagine how effective this type of demonstration can be in your store.

What I'm suggesting you do here is to tap into the power of everyday performance. The demonstration – playing with almost – of products.

Helping customers to visualise your product actually working for them is very powerful.

Customers really are drawn to products when they see life and action around them. Helping customers to visualise your product actually working for them is very powerful. Demonstration does two really significant and useful things for you:

1   Draws customers' attention

2   Makes the store environment feel more dynamic

Both these effects will boost sales.

Making it stick

Over and over we have talked about how the best retailing is down to common sense, passion and gut feel. Out on the streets, market stalls and consumer shows, these components of success are in plentiful supply. They can be seen in the way stallholders price, merchandise, promote and demonstrate. All of the lessons on display can be learned and applied to your store, whether that is a hole-in-the-wall grocers or a 25,000 square foot Currys.

The lychees off Dinesh's stall were delicious by the way. He said that the ones I bought were fresh that morning. So I bought two tubs and as a special deal he did me some kiwi fruit half-price too: lovely.

Case study 15.1 *Smart Retail*: Theatre of lardy dreams

Krispy Kreme stores take three times more money than similarly-sized Dunkin' Donuts stores. Broadly the same product (although KK reckon their recipe delivers a better texture), the same sorts of locations – perhaps Krispy Kreme have a little bit more of an authentic brand heritage, but that's marginal.

So how come they sell so many lovely, lovely, doughnuts? (You can probably work out from my fat head in the picture at the back of this book that I love a doughnut.)

Scott Livengood is the man who took the business from $200 million to $1.2 billion revenues in just three years. His big innovation? The introduction of a little bit of retail theatre. Just like fashion, doughnuts are best when fresh in-store (and hot). Livengood's moment of genius was to connect the childhood delight of hanging around the kitchen when Mum or Dad was baking with the process of buying a doughnut.

Up until Livengood's time, fresh Krispy Kreme doughnuts arrived to customers through an anonymous hatch in the wall, the machinery of cooking that doughnut kept well out of view. Livengood recognised that watching your doughnut cooking in front of you – and taking in the wonderful aroma – would heighten anticipation and spike desire for the product. Stores were then redesigned to make the most of what became 'Doughnut Theatres' and cooking times were changed from early morning to moments that matched customers' optimum desire times – lunchtime and late afternoon. The aromas were then pumped out into the street.

This approach to retail theatre is absolutely relevant – it's about putting exciting products into attractive multi-sensory environments, rescuing products from compartment merchandising and making them live in the minds of customers.

16

Store environment

Layout plays a really important role in the success of your store. Whatever your format, the way in which your store is presented to your customers has a big impact on whether they decide to buy from you or not.

Five jobs the store is doing for you

1 Tempting customers to come in

2 Displaying products

3 Showing off price and promotional displays

4 Leading customers through the different ranges

5 Communicating your store culture.

Look and feel

It's relatively easy these days to create knock-out gorgeous stores at sensible cost. Especially as manufacturers are often rather keen to supply retailers with great-looking free, or part-sponsored, display systems. Looking great is only the start; let's go through the store section-by-section.

> **It's relatively easy these days to create knock-out gorgeous stores at sensible cost.**

Windows

On the high street a good window display is critical. It must be welcoming, it must give passers-by new reasons to come in and it has to be readable in five seconds. Any offers you put in the window should then be easy to locate when the customer comes in looking for them. The best spot for these is on a back wall where they can be seen from the door, yet require the customer to walk the whole length of your store to get to. Doing this exposes customers to more of your store increasing the potential for other sales.

New products are great as window features. When I asked the owner of a successful hardware store how he promoted his hot new items he said 'I put them in the window with a bloody great sign on them that says "bargain" and "brilliant" on it. Customers notice the sign. I know they do because they ask me about these new products and then they buy them.'

Transition zone

This is the area near the door that transfers customers from the outside and then into the store. You have an opportunity here to make or break the customer experience. If the zone is too empty customers can feel exposed and then reluctant to move further into the store. If it's too cluttered that's off-putting too because it makes it hard for customers to get in!

You also need to be aware throughout the store, but here especially, of what retail anthropologist Paco Underhill calls the 'butt-brush factor'. He noticed that customers hate standing anywhere that puts them at risk of other customers constantly brushing past them. In the transition zone this effect can be useful because it keeps people moving forward into the store. It can be a problem in front of displays though, because you want customers to linger in those areas. When they do linger they tend to buy more often. Take a look at all the customer flows in your store, from the entrance and back out again, to see where you can make improvements.

Sales-floor

You need to think about quality, shoplifting, presentation, promotion and customer flow on your sales-floor. There is no magic or right way to set up your space. Have a look at Chapter 3 – the section about reading the store. Then use this technique to shop, shop and shop again. Do it in your own store and those of successful competitors and other successful retailers.

You will soon develop an appreciation of what works and what doesn't. Your eyes and your gut feel are more powerful tools in this than any pre-boxed formats can ever be.

Baskets

If yours is a store where customers ever need to pick up more than one item then you must offer baskets. Customers who pick up a basket nearly always buy something and very often buy more than customers who don't have a basket. Stores always benefit from having baskets available invitingly on the side edges of that transition zone.

Put the baskets higher up, not on the floor. Perching baskets on a table makes it very easy for your customers to just dangle an arm down and almost absent-mindedly pick up a basket. Doing so will increase sales and average transaction values.

Promotional hot-spots

Creative use of promotions is essential. Fill the store with them, show people excellent value and then make it easy for them to take you up on your brilliant offers. Never allow a promotion spot to go empty: if you have run out of a line, even for just a few hours, get the promotion POS off the floor right now. If you don't you will annoy customers who will feel you have let them down.

The ideal promotional hot spots

▶ Visible from the door

▶ Well-lit

▶ Bristling with stock

▶ Easy to linger in front of

▶ Honestly presented

▶ Clearly merchandised

▶ Well-signed

▶ Surprising.

Back wall

Do you remember how record shops always used to feature the Top 20 singles up on the back wall? That was so they could draw every customer right the way through the store. The really savvy stores would make it very easy for customers to walk through the middle of the shop to the back wall, so they would all be flowing down that central aisle. Then when a customer had found their chosen single they would turn and look for the cash desk. This would be placed further back up towards the doors. The customer couldn't easily walk back along the central aisle because it was full of people heading towards them, so they would zigzag through the displays to either side. This zigzagging was brilliant because it meant the customer was exposed to a whole succession of promotional hot-spots at the ends of product racks.

Cash desk

There are lots of arguments over where best to put cash desks. To be honest, all have their pros and cons. My preferred position is halfway down one side wall. You can see most of the store from there, queuing can be dealt with neatly and it doesn't eat into the best selling areas.

The most popular options

▶ Halfway down one side – my favourite

▶ At the front to one side – makes it easy to greet customers walking in but puts the desk right in the middle of important promotional space

▶ In a centre island – although islands can break up sightlines a bit this can work really well, especially if you are able to have two people working the desk most of the time, because the pair can then watch half the store each giving you full visual cover

▶ On the back wall – only popular because it usually puts staff near to back-of-house areas. This makes it hard to greet customers and also makes it the shoplifters' favourite option because staff are so far from the door

Impulse buys

Whatever you sell there will be products in your range that will make great cash-desk impulse purchases. In a newsagent, chocolate is an obvious example. Record shops now put band merchandise, dolls, badges and such, on counters ready for impulse purchase. Anything that is attractive, low-cost and physically small will make a great impulse purchase. Vary your selections a little and don't crowd the till area. A few well-chosen items can have a direct impact on increasing your average transaction values.

> **Anything that is attractive, low-cost and physically small will make a great impulse purchase.**

Sightlines

Two considerations are foremost here:

1   Can customers see their way around the store?
2   Can you see them?

Customers like to be drawn through your space by the exciting and attractive products and promotions you put in their forward vision. Peripheral vision seems to be less important when customers shop. They will often miss things that are right next to them unless you lead them right to the spot.

Being able to see customers is important because it makes it easy for you and the team to acknowledge them. It is also vital in reducing shoplifting. If you can see the thief better they are less able to steal – simple as that.

Signage

Always go for crisp and readable over complex, over-designed or wordy. Customers just do not have the time or inclination to decipher clever or complicated messages. Promotional signage especially should convey a strong, bold message in just a few seconds. Tatty signage does nothing for your store: if a POS gets damaged throw it away or replace it immediately.

Epilogue – and we're done?

Again! That's the second edition read then. Thanks for that, I hope you enjoyed reading *Smart Retail* as much as I did writing it. This is a practical book and I would like to think that you are out there putting this stuff into practice as we speak. Please let me have your feedback on the stuff you didn't like as well as on the bits you've got something out of. Tips on great retailers for me to go and take a look at are always welcome too – especially ones outside the UK or US.

Further *Smart Retail*

Smart Retail speaking

Smart Retail wants to come to your conference or event – I've got a couple of cracking high-energy and practical talks that send delegates away buzzing with ideas.

The *Smart Retail* seminars

Seminars that work – delivering to your managers a new stream of practical ideas, proven strategies and retail techniques that will help them to win the daily sales battle.

The Wednesday clinic

Most Wednesday mornings I give away my time to any retailer who wants a little bit of it on the phone. I'm happy to talk about anything you want: store problems, ideas, opportunities, confusions – anything. I see it as my chance to give back a tiny bit to the industry that's given me so much. I like to talk to as many people as possible each time though, so that means sometimes the conversations might not be able to go on for as long as we'd both maybe like them to. If you want a bit of this time one Wednesday morning send me an email and I'll give you the numbers!

My email address is richard@smart-circle.com and there's more *Smart Retail* at www.Smart-Circle.com.

Thank you for buying and reading *Smart Retail*.

All the best,
Richard

Richard Hammond – Spires Shopping Centre, Barnet
Source: Stillwater Rock

APPENDICES

I   *Take action*

II   *Street Time*

III *Books for retailers*

Take action

Smart Retail is all about the practical. I urge you, please, have a crack at this little personal exercise which is designed to get you started on the route to change. I like selling lots of books but that process is only really rewarding when I hear that readers have actually used them to make positive moves forward. This exercise is a cracking way to kick-start that.

Quickly write down the answers to these four questions. Do it automatically, without over-thinking it. Try to keep writing continuously without pausing. Once you've done that then you can go back over them and do some trimming and tidying. Tackling the exercise this way helps you to be more honest and more practical in your choices.

▶ What five things have jumped out at you from the pages of this book?

▶ What is the first thing you plan to do tomorrow morning?

▶ What objectives will you set for yourself over the rest of the month?

▶ What are the changes you want to see in your own management style this year? How will you make these changes?

Timed plan

And now, more formally, spend a little time filling out this timed plan. Please be honest, stretching and practical.

One month after I finish reading *Smart Retail*, I will have achieved these goals:

1

2

3

4

5

When we get to half-year, these changes will have taken place:

1

2

3

After a year, these important long-term changes will be evident:

1

2

Street Time

This is a day we run as part of our training programmes – normally we obviously try to dress it up a bit with all sorts of important words such as 'structured', 'energising' and 'experiential'. Clients like that sort of guff for some reason. Between you and me: this exercise is about going shopping. It's bloody good fun when done with a group and it always uncovers loads of ideas and gets people thinking creatively too. It can be quite shocking as well – I've had a number of top retailers feed back that they hadn't really seen shops as customers see them in years.

What do we do?

Ideally run it with six people and do it near a high street or a shopping centre. Give each of the delegates twenty quid and a list of five stores they must visit and allow them to choose one other as a 'wildcard'.

Take them through the stuff in *Smart Retail* on:

▶ Reading stores (Chapter 3)

▶ Big Idea (Chapter 4)

▶ Mission and values (Chapter 5)

▶ Discovery (Chapter 14)

Then send them off in teams of two, for two hours, with the explicit brief that they must observe, talk to customers and talk to staff. How they get those conversations going is up to them. They can play-act a bit if they want, whatever. But they must get those conversations going. They can spend their twenty quid however they want – a bit in each store, all at once, whatever.

The hard part

As well as making some specific observations (listed below) they will need to take note of everything with a view to later applying this stuff to the creation of a sector-raiding big idea of their own.

Exercise

Part 1

On returning to the conference room we will be analysing some of the retailers we've looked at against the following criteria:

▶ What is the big idea or mission driving each?

▶ How does that translate into values? (Name five customer emotions per store.)

▶ How are they hanging these things together as part of the overall offer?

▶ What are they doing on discovery?

▶ What evidence can you cite supporting your views on the positioning, added value and differentiation of the store?

Part 2

▶ How might you adapt that offer to better suit the big idea?

▶ What might be a better positioning for that retailer?

Part 3 – long session

As a group: choose one market sector in which you think there might be room to try something new. We will then find our own 'big idea' for a retail entrant into that sector, and then create a business plan for that business.

▶ What will it be called?

▶ What will the store be like?

▶ What's the discovery positioning?

▶ What's the perfect customer experience going to feel like?

▶ Where's the added value?

▶ How will the business be advertised?

▶ What's the mission and what are the values?

▶ How will it find space in the sector?

Run one of these sessions with your team and you will be stunned by what shakes out. Or get in touch with me and we can set one up and run it for you.

Books for retailers

Decent books on retailing are few and far between, which is one of the reasons why I wrote this one. Of those rarities these are the best. Two of the titles are pretty hard to get hold of in the UK but are available on the internet at www.amazon.co.uk. Good bookshops may be able to order them for you too. I've marked the two in question with asterisks.

The Richer Way – Julian Richer (Richer Publishing, 4th ed. 2001)

Richer manages people better than anyone I have ever come across. This is the story of how he does that – essential reading.

Why We Buy – Paco Underhill (Touchstone, 2000)

Retail anthropologist Underhill has an understanding of the habits of shopping that is just breathtaking.

People Don't Buy What You Sell – They Buy What You Stand For – Martin Butler with Simon Gravatt (Management Books, 2000, 2005)

A brilliant combination of personal insight, powerful case studies and loads of revealing interviews with star retailers. This one is another essential for all retailers.

*Retail Success – George Whalin (Willoughby Press, 2001)

George worked in a famous guitar store in 1960s California and has been a leading retail mind ever since. He told me that the moment he realised that he wanted to be a retailer was the first time he sold a customer a guitar package that made both him and the customer smile. I love that.

See Feel Think Do – Andy Milligan and Shaun Smith (Cyan, 2006)

A brilliant book about learning to trust your instincts and to become more proactive in your decision making. Loads of retail case studies – brilliant instinctive retailer Jane Shepherdson says it best in her endorsement for this book: 'The sooner we start acting on our instincts, and listening less to business school theories, the more the customer will benefit.'

Made in America, My Story – Sam Walton (Bantam Books, 1992)

The story of how Sam Walton and his team built the world's biggest company: Wal-Mart. This is a lot of fun, full of breathtaking daring, down-home philosophy and some great retail stories. An absolute must-have.

Uncommon Practice – Andy Milligan and Shaun Smith (Prentice Hall, 2002)

Absolutely fantastic set of case studies that tell the inside story of 19 brands that are each brilliant at delivering great customer service. Bloody expensive but worth it, especially as Andy and Shaun resist the temptation to over-edit or to spin too much interpretation onto the raw material.

INDEX

Page numbers in *italics* denote photographs, figures and tables.

action-planning 4
added value 110–12
advertising 137–9, 140–2
  catalogues 141–2
  in changing rooms 127
  posters 141
  print 141
  radio 140
  simple 137–9
  TV 140–1
  see also marketing
Advertising Association 140–1
Alexander, H. 120
Amazon 88
Anthropologie, customer service 101–2
Apple Store, format-led discovery 179–80
arcades 153–4
area manager xxi–xxii
assistant store manager (ASM) xxi
  as 'keeper' of store culture 31
average transaction value 175

B&Q, promotion-led discovery 177
Baird, J.L. 167
balloon day 66–7
bargains 118–20, 133–4
  democracy of 120–1
behaviours 50–1

Big Idea 23–6, 34
  delivery 95
Blériot, L. 167
Blink (Gladwell) 74
Bon Marché 155–7, *156*
book retailers 88
book signings 130
books on retailing 207–8
Boots, promotion-led discovery 177
Boucicaut, A. 155
brand 24, 137
  loyalty 173
branded product 132
Branson, R. 46
breakout retailers xv
British Empire, mission statement 34–5
Brooker, C. 138
browsing 156
Butler, M. 23
buy now pay later 133
buy one get one free 129

Calton, R. 5
Carphone Warehouse xvii, 40–1
  service-led discovery 178
catalogue advertising 141–2
catalogue-based mail order 150
Caudwell, J. 41
celebrity visit 130
chains, retail 150, 152
change 13–14

benefit, effort and cost 18
exercise 202–3
charity giving 131
children's competitions 127
Christie, L. 4–5
Coca-Cola Company 71–3
New Coke 72–3
Cohen, A. 145, *146*
Colgate 85
colleagues, and improvement 77–9
Comet 115–18
community events 127
community markets 151
commuting 153
competition, price 114
consistency 96
consumption 121–3
The Container Store 97
service-led discovery 178
conversion rate 174–5
cost savings 29
cost-cutting 165
cost-led strategy 107, 114–18
everyday low prices (ELP)
115–16
merchant dealing 116–17
price competition 114
costs, and improvement 79–81
culture
of improvement 74–5
store 31
customer 83–169
at centre 62
emotions 36
experiences xi, 88
first visit advantage 85–6
and improvement 75–6
loyalty 85
observation 15

questioning 16–18
service 91–105
traffic 167
training 117–18
customer service 91–105
Anthropologie 101–2
Big Idea delivery 95
consistency 96
discovery need 95
Elif Restaurant (Liverpool) 101
employee satisfaction 95
feedback 96
Focus DIY 102
great moments 98–105
honesty and openness 96–7
improved 29–30
Lush 98–9
respect 97
sales commission 97
service quality initiatives 91–2
Shoe Clinic 103–5
simplicity 95
Specsavers 99–100
The Warehouse 100
Victoria's Secret 102–3
customer-get-customer 128

Data Protection Act 143–4
database marketing 142–7
email 142–3
measurement 146–7
postcards 144–5
decision-making tools 19
Degg, N. 93
delegation
power 59
responsibility 59
demonstration 189–90
department store 150, 155–7

differentiated strategy 107–8
discount off future purchase 132
discovery 173–86
    benefits of leading by 174–5
    different types 175–86
    format-led 179–82
    need 95
    product-led 182–6
    promotion-led 175–7
    service-led 177–8
displays in empty stores 126
Dunstone, C. xvii

easyJet, logo 137
economic growth xiii
Elif Restaurant (Liverpool),
    customer service 101
email database marketing 142–3
emotions test 36–7
employee satisfaction 95
enjoyment 30–1
everyday low prices (ELP) 115–16,
    119
expansion 159

favouritism 65
fear, management by 41, 42–3, 57
feedback 61, 96
financial rewards 56–7
Firebox, format-led discovery 181
first visit advantage 85–6
Focus DIY, customer service 102
footfall 174
format xi, 109
format-led discovery 179–82
    Apple Store 179–80
    Firebox 181
    Lush 181
    Pret a Manger 180–1
    Target 180
    Urban Outfitters 181–2
forming an opinion 10
freebies 65–6
fun 30–1, 38–40
    with job descriptions 38–40
    value of 39

generalists 109
Gerrard, A. 157
gift certificate promotions 132–3
Gilman, G. 158–60
Gladwell, M. 74
Great Atlantic and Pacific Tea
    Company (A&P) 158–60, 159
greeter 165
Groceteria 157
Gruen, V. 154
gut feel 73–4

Habitat, product-led discovery 183
Harrods 24, 120
Hartford, G. 158–60
heroes board 52
Hillam, A. 110
history of retail 149–69
honest pricing 119
honesty and openness 96–7
Hotel Chocolat 23–4
Human Resources (HR) 28–9

ideas
    improvement 70
    programme 10
IKEA 25–6, 162–4, 163
ILVA 25–6
    product-led discovery 183–4
implied sanction 57–8
improvement 69–70, 74–81

and colleagues 77–9
and costs 79–81
culture of 74–5
and customers 75–6
ideas 70
and you 76–7
see also performance
improvement
impulse buys 197
incentive programmes 63
independents 109–10
indoor town centre shopping
153–4
Industrial Revolution 153
information sharing 59
interest-free credit 133
Internet 150
retailing xi–xii
inventions in retail 149–50

JFDI management style 42–3
John Lewis Partnership, service-led
discovery 178
joint activity 126

Kamprad, I. 162–4
KFC, and 20-second ceremony
53–4
King, J. xvi–xvii
Kingfisher companies 115
Krispy Kreme 190–1
Krok, R. 46

leadership 28–9
definition 29
Leahy, Sir T. 36, 88
Leonard, S. 174, 184–6
listening 60–1
Livengood, S. 191

Lloyds TSB 93
Lo Kass 152
local radio broadcasts 132
location 109
loyalty programmes 128
Lush
customer service 98–9
format-led discovery 181

McDonalds 138
MacLaurin, Lord 36
mail order, catalogue-based 150
malls 153–4
management 27
by fear 41, 42–3, 57
JFDI 42–3
people 27
manager
area xxi–xxii
store xiv, xx, 92
marketing 137–47
database 142–7
email 142–3
four 'P's 139
postcards 144–5
questions chain 139–40
theory 139–40
see also advertising
markets, community 151
measurement trap 70–3
meeting place 131
megamalls 154–5
merchandising 188
merchant dealing 116–17
merchants 151
Microsoft Excel 146
Milligan, A. 74
mission 27–8, 33–40
statement 34–40

mistakes 45–6, 163–4
motivation 48, 55–68
  components of 55–6
  financial reward 56–7
  implied sanction 57–8
  non-financial rewards 62–6
  self-respect 58–62

needs 112–14
  exercises 112–14
non-financial rewards 52, 62–6
  balloon day 66–7
  team ballot 65
Northgate Shopping Center, Seattle
  154

observable positive behaviours
  50–1
observation
  basic store components 15–16
  customer 15
  stores 14–18
on-shelf availability xvi–xvii
one-to-ones, successful 58
Orange 138
original equipment manufacturer
  (OEM) 116

passion 6–7
Patel, M. 6–7
people management 27
Pepsi 71–3
  Challenge 71–3
percentage off 129
performance delivery 11
performance improvement 13, 27
  four rules of 87
  and promotions *135*
  see also improvement

personal goals 1–5
Phones 4U 41
Piggly Wiggly 157
Pink Palace 157
pioneers of retail 158–69
place 139
play.com, promotion-led discovery
  176
point of sale (POS) 188
postcard database marketing 144–5
poster advertising 141
power
  delegation of 59
  of wonder 167
Powerhouse 92
praise 48–9
Pret a Manger, format-led discovery
  180–1
price 24, 139, 165
  competition 114
pricing
  honest 119
  logic 188–9
Primark 120
print advertising 141
product 139
  branded 132
product personality 138
product-led discovery 182–6
  Habitat 183
  ILVA 183–4
  Top Shop 183
profile raising 9–11
promotion 139
  vocal 187–8
promotion-led discovery 175–7
  B&Q 177
  Boots 177
  play.com 176

Tesco 176
promotions 125–35
  adverts in changing rooms 127
  bargains 133–4
  book signings 130
  branded product 132
  buy now pay later 133
  buy one get one free 129
  celebrity visit 130
  charity giving 131
  children's competitions 127
  community events 127
  customer-get-customer 128
  discount off future purchase 132
  displays in empty stores 126
  gift certificate 132–3
  interest-free credit 133
  joint activity 126
  local radio broadcasts 132
  loyalty programmes 128
  lunch at the store 130–31
  meeting place 131
  percentage off 129
  and performance improvement
    135
  planner 134
  sampler clubs 129
  seminars 131
  special nights 129–30
  sponsorship 127
  storecards 133
  surveys 130
  tip sheets 127–8

questioning
  customer 16–18
  staff 16

radio advertising 140

Radio Advertising Bureau (RAB)
  140
recognition 28, 47–54, 67–8
  20-second ceremony 51–3, 54
  bad habits 49–50
  good habits 50
  heroes board 52
respect 27–8, 40–7, 97
responsibility, delegation 59
retail
  chains 150, 152
  great inventions in 149–50
  history of 149–69
  pioneers 158–69
retailer
  book 88
  breakout xv
retailing, books on 207–8
rewards
  financial 56–7
  inappropriate 63
  non-financial 52, 62–6
Richer, J. 31, 69
Richer Sounds, logo 137
The Richer Way (Richer) 69
risk 44–5

Sainsbury's xvi–xvii, 36
sales assistant xiv
sales commission 97
sampler clubs 129
sanction, implied 57–8
Saunders, C. 157
See Feel Think (Milligan and Smith)
  74
Segel, R. 126
segment-focused strategy 108
self-respect 58–62
self-service 157–8, *158*

Selfridge, G. 166–9, *168*
Selfridges & Co 24, 166–9
seminars 131
service profit chain 31–3, *32*, 37
service quality xi
   initiatives 91–2
service-led discovery 177–8
   Carphone Warehouse 178
   John Lewis Partnership 178
   The Container Store 178
Shepherdson, J. 44–5
Shoe Clinic, customer service
   103–5
shopping
   indoor town centre 153–4
   malls 153–4
simplicity xvi–xviii, 13–14, 95,
   107–23
Smalling-Archer, J. 69
Smart Retail
   seminars 199
   speaking 199
Smith, S. 74
special nights 129–30
specialising 10
specialists 109
Specsavers, customer service
   99–100
sponsorship 127
staff
   behaviour 167
   questioning 16
store 171–97
   back wall 196
   basic components 15–16
   baskets 195
   cash desk 196
   culture 31
   department 150, 155–7

   environment 193–7
   impulse buys 197
   layout 193
   lunch at 130–1
   manager xiv, xx, 92
   observation 14–18
   owner xx
   promotional hot-spots 195
   sales-floor 194–5
   sightlines 197
   signage 197
   transition zone 194
   windows 193–4
storecards 133
strategy 107–23
   cost-led 107
   differentiated 107–8
   segment-focused 108
street time 17–18, 40, 204–6
success, celebration of 62
support 30
surprise 173
surveys 130
sustainability 121–3

Target 24, 164
   format-led discovery 180
Taylor, D. 69
team 21–81
   ballot 65
   happy 27
   meetings 51–3, 67–8
   member xx–xxi
Tesco 9
   mission statement and values
     36–7
   promotion-led discovery 176
'thank you' moments 51
'thank you' notes 51–3

Thorntons 23
timed plan 202–3
tip sheets 127–8
TNT 34, 69
  mission statement 34
Top Shop 44–5
  big idea 44
  product-led discovery 183
traders 187–8
training
  customer 117–18
  encouragement 59
transaction values 88
TV advertising 140–1

Uncommon Practice (Milligan and
  Smith) 88
Underhill, P. 173
unemployment 42
Up Against the Wal-Marts (Taylor and
  Smalling-Archer) 69
Urban Outfitters, format-led
  discovery 181–2

value 24, 25–6, 118–20
  added 110–12
values 35–40
  in action 38

transaction 88
Vanity Fair 168
Victoria's Secret, customer service
  102–3
visioning 4–5
vocal promotion 187–8
volunteering 9

Wal-Mart 23, 24, 115, 119, 164–6
  Visitor Center *166*
Walton, S. 23, 115, 164–6
  customer genius 164–5
The Warehouse, customer service
  100
Wednesday clinic 199
Whalin, G. 46
Whitechapel Road, London 187–8
Whole Foods Market (WFM)
  122–3
WHSmith 25
  High Street 25
  Travel 25
Why We Buy (Underhill) 173
wonder, power of 167
Woolworth Building, New York
  City 161, *161*
Woolworth, F.W. 160–2
Woolworths 160–2